Crucible of Fire

Crucible of Fire

The Church Confronts Apartheid

Edited by
Jim Wallis
and
Joyce Hollyday

ORBIS BOOKS
Maryknoll, New York

SOJOURNERS
Washington, D.C.

The Catholic Foreign Mission Society of America (Maryknoll) recruits and trains people for overseas missionary service. Through Orbis Books, Maryknoll aims to foster the international dialogue that is essential to mission. The books published, however, reflect the opinions of their authors and are not meant to represent the official position of the society.

To Allan, Jr., Pulane, Belen, and Leineke Boesak—
and all the children of South Africa—
who hold the future in their hands

Alas, my country! Thou wilt have no need
of enemy to bring thee to thy doom . . .
For not alone by war a nation falls.
Though she be fair, serene as radiant morn,
Though girt by seas, secure in armament,
Let her but spurn the vision of the Cross;
Tread with contemptuous feet on its command
Of Mercy, Love and Human Brotherhood,
And she some fateful day, shall have no need
Of enemy to bring her to the dust.

Some day, though distant it may be—with God
A thousand years are but as yesterday—
The germs of hate, injustice, violence,
Like an insidious canker in the blood,
Shall eat the nation's vitals. She shall see
Break forth the blood-red tide of anarchy,
Sweeping her plains, laying her cities low,
And bearing on its seething, crimson flood
The wreck of Government, of home, and all
The nation's pride, its splendour and its power.
On, with relentless flow, into the seas
Of God's eternal vengeance wide and deep.
But for God's grace! Oh may it hold thee fast,
My country, until justice shall prevail
O'er wrong and o'er oppression's cruel power,
And all that makes humanity to mourn.

—Sol Plaatjie
South Africa, 1913

Contents

Foreword

Allan Boesak

Immediately following the election of George Bush as president of the United States, an editorial appeared in one of the South African newspapers, commenting on the significance of the victory. It read in part, "The forces against apartheid in the West have been called to a halt, and the policies of the previous administration will be continued." Gleefully, the writer concluded by saying, "The government of South Africa has a friend in the White House again."

As I have travelled around the world and through many regions of the United States of America, I have met many people from all walks of life. I have met with business leaders, scholars, attorneys, and countless church leaders. They are always eager to ask questions about what is happening inside of South Africa. They raise honest concerns about the struggle for freedom and the South African government's cruel recalcitrance.

They listen attentively to the reports of government repression embodied in countless arrests and the detention of anyone the police suspect to be a lover of freedom. They learn how children barely old enough to know the rules of football are hauled into jail, interrogated for treason, and often detained for weeks on end. As they listen, regardless of their position in society, be they rich or poor, believer or nonbeliever, they all seem to feel a deep sense of sympathy for the victims and a growing outrage against the apartheid system, which daily attempts to break the backs of those who merely desire to live in a free and democratic South Africa.

True, our friends may not live in the White House; but those who are struggling for freedom in South Africa have countless friends in the United States. They are people of conscience whose basic respect for human dignity prohibits any toleration of the barbaric notions of racial superiority to which the apartheid regime so doggedly clings.

Some friends of the freedom movement in South Africa are people who fought against the terrible horrors of Nazism. Many of them remember how high the final price was in stopping the fanatics of that era, supremacists who refused to bow to reasonable discourse.

As these friends listen to reports from South Africans today, one can almost see in their faces the flashbacks of an era they had hoped was past—a time they prayed would never come again. As they listen, the realization of history beginning to repeat itself sparks an inner flame of resolve in them—a burning desire to end the evil before it spreads any further.

They may not work in the White House, but they become faithful friends of ours because many of them have experienced firsthand the injustices of racism in their own land. And they know how fragile freedom becomes when bigotry obtains the official blessing of the powers of state.

They may not be political analysts or experts in theories of governance, but they do understand the fundamental requisite of any true democracy—one person, one vote. They may not sit in the Oval Office and sip tea in the Rose Garden, but they do know the difference between right and wrong, good and evil, justice and injustice. Because of this, they are our friends. They have not lost that God-given capacity to discern a righteous cause. They are wise enough to know that the powers of greed and hatred and violence, when left unchecked, threaten us all.

With or without the White House, they are our friends, and their number grows with each passing hour. Each day Nelson Mandela is locked behind bars, we grieve—but we gain more friends across the globe. Each time a child is imprisoned, we mourn—but the world rushes to our aid, offering new forms of support and prayer. With every drop of innocent blood shed in our struggle for justice, we cry out—but the movement strengthens in its resolve to endure the pain until freedom is a reality for all.

Indeed, we have many friends—despite what the South African newspapers say, and regardless of the policies of this or that U.S. administration. These friends are growing sick and tired of the demonic evils wrought by apartheid's pharaohs. They, like the oppressed masses in South Africa, are rising up and saying, "Enough is enough!"

When their collective power is mobilized in the churches, in the labor unions, in the schools and universities, and in the streets, the groundswell will be such that President Bush will have to listen. He will be forced to face his own historic complicity with the perpetrators of evil in South Africa. Our friends upon whom he depends for re-election will offer him no other alternative but to rethink his relationship with the government of South Africa and end all forms of U.S. support for that terrorist and illegitimate power.

Then those of us who are struggling for freedom in South Africa may discover a new friend in the White House. Conversion, even of the staunchest foe, is always possible. But in this case, Mr. Bush will have to be born again. No half-conversion will help.

Pundits of reform who want merely to soften apartheid are like swabbies rearranging the deck furniture on the Titanic. The ship of apartheid cannot sail for long. The time has come to abandon ship—to dismantle apartheid once and for all. No amount of patchwork reformism can save it. The vision of a free South Africa has ripped an irreparable hole in apartheid's hull, and it is sinking like a stone.

Let there be no mistake about it—apartheid is going under and will take with it any who choose to cling to it too long. That is why President Bush must completely break with the past policies of Ronald Reagan. "Constructive engagement" is destructive engagement.

To all who choose to stand with apartheid, the news must go forth—do not blame us when some day you find yourselves standing on the wrong side of history. We have tried to warn you, but you have not listened.

Nothing can stop the tide once it is set in motion. In South

Africa today, a tidal wave for freedom is rising. It will eventually wash away any vestige of the segregated society we so rightly abhor.

Freedom is coming. It is inevitable. It would be inevitable even if it were merely a political movement. Yet, it is so much more than that.

The struggle for freedom in South Africa has dimensions beyond mere politics. There is a spiritual force at work in this struggle. And because the fields have been moistened with the blood of so many martyrs, a gathering cloud of communing saints energizes our efforts.

Ultimately, this is a movement of faith, and that is why the government so fears us. In the end, faith is always more powerful than the mightiest military. Guns can rust and bullets run out, but faith persists; and it shall win the day.

The leaders of apartheid accuse us of being unfaithful because we are political. What they fail to see is that we are political because we are faithful. If we were not faithful, we could turn our backs on the suffering and oppression and accept apartheid as it is today.

But being faithful, we know that God never intended any persons to spend their days in the wretched filth of a squatter camp, separated from loved ones and laboring without a just wage. Because we are faithful, we know that God never condones one group to wallow in excess while others slowly starve to death. Because we are faithful, we know how God wants us to live. It is the unfaithful who continually violate God's laws by constructing positions of privilege that deny others a basic chance to live safely and happily with those they love.

Moses was political when he confronted Pharaoh. Why? Because Moses was faithful. Pharaoh was the unfaithful one. Amos was political when he confronted the corrupt leaders of his day. Why? Because Amos was faithful. Those he decried were the unfaithful ones. Jesus was political when he dared to disrupt the temple tax system and declared the temple to be a house of prayer. Why? Because he was faithful. The collaborators with the Roman occupational forces were the unfaithful ones, despite their self-proclaimed religiosity.

Yes, we are political, but it is because we are first faithful.

Holding to the faith of the gospel of Christ gives us no option save that of risking life and limb in this struggle for righteousness in our land. We cannot but be political given the demands of the gospel which are so shamefully assaulted by apartheid at every turn.

Our friends are political, too. Why? Because they are also people of faith who respect the God-ordained vision of justice emerging in the black churches of South Africa today. Our friends have read the Bible, and they have gone to Sunday School, and they see quite clearly who in this situation is doing the work of God and who is doing the devil's business.

They know that Jesus was a poor man who lived simply within the communities of the poor. They know that he had little patience with the power-brokers of his day and dared to face their wrath rather than give up his vision of a new way. Just as he could not be intimidated by threats of violence and death, our friends see in our struggle the same spirit of determination and resolve that will not be stopped, no matter how difficult the path may be.

Freedom is coming to South Africa. There is no doubting this fact. The churches know it, even if the governments do not.

The time is at hand for the people of faith to stand with us in this historic struggle. The cost will be high, but higher still would be the price paid for our unfaithfulness in a day of urgency and trial. Let all people of faith be as one. Let us stand for truth in the crucible of fire until South Africa is free.

Acknowledgments

Our first thanks must go to all the brothers and sisters across South Africa who welcomed us into their homes and shared their stories. Their hope in the midst of tremendous suffering has called us again to the gospel's promises and given us encouragement to carry on. We especially want to thank the Boesak family—Allan, Dorothy, Lieneke, Belen, Pulane, and Allan, Jr.—for their gracious hospitality throughout our stay and for the reminder that the bonds of love cannot be severed by even the most severe threats.

Most of this book first appeared in *Sojourners* magazine, and we are grateful to the entire staff for patience and support on the project. Special recognition goes to Michael Curry, who put in long hours overseeing the project and bringing it to completion. We also want to thank LeAnne Moss, who transcribed the many hours of tapes we brought back from South Africa; Michael Verchot and Mary Teresa McCullagh, who did final preparation on the manuscript; and Suzanne St. Yves, Ella Curry, Joe Lynch, Karen Lattea, Michael Airhart, Jim Miller, Scot DeGraf, and Jim Rice, who all pitched in with whatever was needed to see that the project was completed.

And finally, we extend our warm thanks to Robert Ellsberg and all the others at Orbis Books whose flexibility and commitment made the book possible at this crucial time in South Africa.

Introduction

Jim Wallis and Joyce Hollyday

At 1:10 on the morning of August 31, 1988, an expertly set bomb exploded in Khotso House, located in the center of Johannesburg, South Africa. The name "Khotso House" means "The House of Peace." Structural damage was extensive, as the building collapsed in upon itself.

We had visited Khotso House a few months before and found a building bustling with energy and activity. It housed the headquarters of the South African Council of Churches (SACC) as well as offices of human rights, trade union, and detainee support groups. Everyone in Khotso House was deeply engaged in the struggle against apartheid and on behalf of a new South Africa.

Just six weeks after the Khotso House attack, a firebomb destroyed Khana House, the office of the South African Council of Catholic Bishops. These bombings—along with previous attacks against church, union, and community groups—remain officially unsolved.

After the attack on Khotso House, we spoke by phone with Reverend Frank Chikane, general secretary of the SACC. Chikane told us, "This is connected to the witness and action of the churches."

A few months before, on February 24, 1988, the South African government had outlawed the activities of seventeen anti-apartheid organizations, including the two-million-member United Democratic Front and the Congress of South African Trade Unions, the nation's largest labor federation. The meaning of the action was clear: any opposition to the white regime would no longer be tolerated; peaceful protest against apartheid was ordered to stop.

Twenty months of a government-imposed state of emergency had already seriously crippled some anti-apartheid groups, with many members suffering detention, police violence, and death. The government's forced exile of the media from black townships and other conflict areas had effectively turned out the lights, keeping the rest of the world from seeing what was happening in South Africa.

With the February 24 bannings, the consolidation of totalitarian rule and the creation of a virtual police state were complete. The intended effect of the government repression was to engineer a state in which there would be no one left to protest.

Four days later, on Sunday, February 28, Reformed Church minister Reverend Allan Boesak preached in his church in Cape Town on Jesus' response to the threats and intimidations of state power, choosing Luke 13:31–35 as his text. The religious leaders of Jesus' day counseled caution and retreat in the face of Herod's threats, but Jesus chose confrontation, saying, "Go and tell that fox. . . ." The term "fox" was one of particular derision in Jesus' day, and his meaning was unmistakably clear. Also clear was the reason for a black South African pastor's reference to Jesus' words two thousand years later.

On Monday, February 29, Allan Boesak, Archbishop Desmond Tutu, Frank Chikane, and scores of other church leaders led hundreds in a prayer service and march on the South African Parliament, to demand the restoration of the right of peaceful protest. In the spirit of nonviolent civil disobedience, as exemplified by Gandhi and Martin Luther King, Jr., they refused to disperse and retreat when confronted by a menacing line of riot police, but calmly knelt in prayer. The clergy were detained by the police, strictly warned, and then released, while hundreds of other marchers were hosed down with police water cannons.

After their release the church leaders vowed to continue confronting the South African authorities and promised that the march was only the beginning. "We are not defying, we are obeying; and we are going to obey God every day," said Archbishop Tutu. In the United States, ABC News anchor Peter

Jennings announced, "In South Africa the church has taken up the burden of the people." Thus was born a new era in the conflict between church and state in South Africa that still dominates the country today.

The spiritual commitment and political determination of the marchers flew in the face of others claiming the name of Christ in South Africa. Many in the government, including State President P. W. Botha, prevail on their Dutch Reformed faith to justify apartheid as God's will. The exchange of theological claims between Botha and the church leaders reached a fever pitch in the weeks following the March to Parliament.

Although Tutu, Boesak, Chikane, Beyers Naudé, and other church leaders have played a key role in the anti-apartheid struggle for many years, they now face a unique trial and opportunity. At this moment in history, the church in South Africa remains one of the few institutions with any means of working for peaceful change. And the church leaders have accepted the challenge.

In the political vacuum created by the silencing of the other groups, the churches have moved to the front lines of the freedom struggle, calling for a campaign of massive nonviolent direct action aimed at the system of apartheid. They are armed only with the moral force and promises of the gospel—and the deeply imbedded hope that South Africa will one day be free.

For years we had hoped and prayed to go to South Africa, but we couldn't find a way. Then in March 1988, unexpectedly, a way opened up for us, just two weeks after the Parliament March. It was a rare privilege to be eyewitnesses to the church's courage and determination as the drama in the church-state conflict unfolded.

We went to South Africa at the longstanding invitation of Allan Boesak. We were hosted throughout the country principally by the country's black church leadership. That perspective is therefore strongly reflected in these pages.

The role of South African women should also be noted at this point. For although they have not emerged as upfront church leaders—for reasons rooted in both culture and church— women have provided a strong stream of resistance for many decades in South Africa. Their story could—and should—be the subject of another book.

During our forty-day sojourn across South Africa, we were graciously welcomed into homes and church services, rallies and strategy sessions. In squatter camps and townships and migrant hostels, from Cape Town to Johannesburg to Pretoria, in Crossroads and Soweto and King Williams Town, from Durban to Pietermaritzburg to East London, we listened and gathered up the pieces of the story of this troubled land. Our days were full, intense, and rich in both breadth and depth of contact with people and events—a rare opportunity for which we are deeply grateful.

Much of what we carried home with us first appeared in the pages of *Sojourners*. But there was much more that we felt needed to be shared, beyond the limited space of a magazine. This book is a sort of "snapshot" of a moment in history, a moment that is critical for understanding the ongoing struggle and the evolving future of South Africa.

The issues at stake in South Africa are quite simple and at the same time very complicated; we recognize that to write about them is a risky thing. Our time in South Africa had both the personally transforming power of an in-depth experience and all the limitations of a brief stay. While we were treated as friends, we remain outsiders like anyone who does not walk in the shoes of those who must carry on the struggle every day. Those in the midst of the conflict, interviewed in depth in these pages, provide the best background, analysis, and vision for the future.

They—and the people who follow them—are the ones who ultimately must pay the price for their commitment to the gospel and their compassion for this anguished land. Having long ago exhausted all of its moral resources, the only weapon the white South African government has left is violence. Any serious strategy of nonviolent resistance on the part of the churches will cost the lives of some—perhaps many—who will bring down upon themselves the brutality of a government losing its grip.

After the bombing of Khotso House, the police closed the building and took control of the SACC headquarters. SACC workers are "squatters" now, according to Frank Chikane; activities are continuing from a variety of offices around Johannesburg where they were taken in.

If the purpose of the bombing was to distract and disrupt the South African Council of Churches and to make it more difficult for it to carry out its work, the attack succeeded. But if the attack was meant to intimidate and turn back the churches from the risky path they have chosen, those who planted the bomb and those who gave the orders will be sorely disappointed. "We have no doubt that the forces of evil are arranging themselves against the church in South Africa," said Chikane at a news conference following the bombing. "But we intend to continue telling the truth."

The truth seems to get clearer every day. The white South African government's policy of reform is a sham. The only changes have been cosmetic, failing to deal with the central issue of political power, which remains entirely in white hands.

Meanwhile, the oppressive brutality of the Pretoria regime has steadily grown. With successive states of emergency, government crackdowns, the elimination of a free press, massive detentions, uncontrolled police violence, and the banishing of the international media, South Africa has virtually become a military dictatorship and a terrorist state.

If the white government does not respond to the moral initiative now being undertaken by the churches by beginning a process of real political change, more serious confrontation will follow. And it will be costly. If the "moderate" or "liberal" forces in white Afrikanerdom don't act soon to try to prevent the inevitable catastrophe, their time will pass forever. As the ruling powers continue to harden, crush all democratic possibilities, define "reform" only on their terms, and rely on their preferred military options, the conflict only deepens.

There is now the real possibility of a martyred church in South Africa. That reality places a new responsibility on the rest of the church worldwide. A suffering church has a moral claim on the rest of the body of Christ.

No one from the outside can make the choice of costly resistance for the South African churches; they must accept that calling for themselves. But we will need to stand alongside, raise

our voices, offer ourselves in resistance, and commit our resources as never before.

The United States, along with Britain and West Germany,
plays a particularly crucial role in South Africa. Comprehensive
political and economic sanctions against the white regime in Pretoria would make a critical difference. At the present, none of
these governments has the will to make a decisive commitment.
The most vicious racism on the globe, enforced by increasing totalitarianism, doesn't stir the heart of official Washington like its
own ideological obsessions with other parts of the world.

The magnitude of the hypocrisy and injustice in South Africa
would certainly have called forth the pronouncements of the
Old Testament prophets. It should indeed fire the faith of the
American churches. The more we see our sisters and brothers
suffer, the more we need to look at ourselves.

The question before us now is not simply what the South
African churches can do, but what we are prepared to do. The
South African churches have launched a campaign aimed at
removing the apartheid regime. That courageous effort deserves
and desperately needs unequivocal international support.

The white South African government must clearly understand
that to attack the South African churches is to attack the whole
body of Christ. If that is not yet clear to Pretoria, it is our
responsibility to make it clear. The time has come for the faith,
prayers, and energy of the worldwide church of Jesus Christ to
be clearly focused on bringing an end to the diabolical system
known as apartheid.

The day of freedom in South Africa is certainly coming, but
the price of freedom will be high. The South African churches
have counted the cost and are asking for our solidarity. The days
ahead will be critical, and the world will be watching. Who will
stand up in the South African churches? And who around the
world will stand up with them?

*Frank Chikane stands outside Khotso House, headquarters of the
South African Council of Churches, the morning after the bombing.*

Allan Boesak under arrest: "The time has come to call apartheid by its true name—a sin."

1

Into the Crucible of Fire: The Church Steps forward in South Africa

Jim Wallis

St. George's Cathedral was packed to overflowing. A rally had been planned to launch the newly formed Committee to Defend Democracy, an organization hastily put together by church leaders to protest the South African government's recent assault on democratic groups. But just hours before, the rally was banned, along with the three-day-old organization itself. Quickly, a service was called to take place in the cathedral at the same hour the banned rally would have been held.

Despite government efforts to obstruct communication, word of the service had gotten around. Police roadblocks had been set up to keep the young people from the black townships from getting to the church service in downtown Cape Town, but many made it anyway, surging into the sanctuary like a powerful river of energy, determination, and militant hope.

There was no more room to sit or stand in the whole church. People were everywhere—in the aisles, the choir lofts, and the spaces behind and in front of the pulpit. People of all human colors waited for the worship to begin and the word to be preached. Outside the cathedral, the riot police were massing.

It was our first day in South Africa. The March 13th cathedral service provided a dramatic introduction to our forty-day sojourn in this land of sorrow and hope. Indeed, the notes struck in St. George's that day would be the recurring themes in the weeks that followed.

"The battle is on!" thundered Allan Boesak in his bright red and black robe, "but Jesus Christ is Lord!" Applause and shouts of affirmation rang out as the preacher exclaimed, "The government of South Africa has signed its own death warrant. No government can take on God and survive. That is the good news for the people of South Africa and the bad news for the South African government!"

Archbishop Desmond Tutu preached that, even when all looks hopeless, "We must assert, and assert confidently, that God is in charge." He was fiery and strong as he told the white rulers who enforce the brutal system of apartheid, "You are not God, you are mortals. It is God whom we worship, and God cannot be mocked. You have already lost. Come and join the winning side!"

The "recessional" for this service turned into a chanting stampede of young people singing freedom songs. The conflict between the church and the state in South Africa had escalated.

The recent round of confrontation had begun two weeks before when, in an unprecedented display of unity, twenty-five church leaders, along with five hundred clergy and laity, marched to the South African Parliament in Cape Town carrying a petition which demanded the restoration of the right of peaceful protest. The February 29, 1988, "Parliament March" was in response to the South African government's action on February 24, which effectively banned seventeen organizations that had been leading the struggle against apartheid and which restricted the nation's largest labor federation from political activity.

With the government's silencing of major organizations such as the two-million-member United Democratic Front (UDF) and the Congress of South African Trade Unions (COSATU), the church leaders felt compelled to act in a new and unified way. Their action was met with water cannons and arrests. And it set into motion a chain of events that dominated the attention of the country for weeks and signaled a new stage in the struggle for freedom in South Africa, one in which the churches would play a central role.

Like all conflicts, this one is very personal for those involved. This was underscored for us by our experiences in the Boesaks' home, which was our home base for the almost six weeks we traveled throughout South Africa. Extraordinary events were occurring almost daily for the Boesak family, but somehow, by the grace of God, the stuff of ordinary human and family life continued, and, in fact, became a saving grace.

Two nights before we arrived, a brick had been thrown through the living room window. The next morning, the death threats over the phone began in earnest; they would continue regularly through the first two weeks we were there.

Later that week Boesak invited me to accompany him to Pretoria for the Federal Council Meeting of the Dutch Reformed Church, which takes place every two years. It was with the help of the white Dutch Reformed Church that the idea of apartheid was originally conceived and given religious justification. Membership in the highest circles of Afrikaner power and the white Dutch Reformed Church are virtually synonymous.

The Dutch Reformed Church is strictly divided into racial categories; the issue over which the powerful white leaders had finally divided the church was, ironically enough, communion. White worshipers refused to drink from the same cup as their black brothers and sisters.

The Federal Council meeting brought together delegates from the four branches of the Dutch Reformed Church—black, so-called colored, Indian, and white—whose strictly separated racial constituencies mirror the divisions that define virtually everything about South African life and society. The white Dutch Reformed Church likes to think of itself as the mother church spawning new churches for the purpose of mission. In reality, the white Dutch Reformed Church has been the ruling church, creating dependent and subservient branches to enforce racial segregation and maintain white control.

In recent years, however, that control has been seriously challenged by the increasingly independent and spiritually revitalized black churches in South Africa's Dutch Reformed "family."

In particular, the Dutch Reformed Mission Church has mounted a powerful theological attack on apartheid as a false and secular gospel which is completely contrary to the gospel of Jesus Christ.

At its historic Ottawa meeting in 1982, the World Alliance of Reformed Churches (the seventy-million-member world communion of which all of South Africa's Dutch Reformed Churches were once a part) dramatically acted in declaring apartheid a heresy, expelling the white Dutch Reformed Church, and electing Allan Boesak as its new president. In 1986 Boesak was elected moderator of the Dutch Reformed Mission Church in South Africa, whose confession, which all members must sign, now names apartheid a sin against the gospel and a heresy in the church. The dynamic and prophetic role undertaken by the black churches and the entrenched resistance of the white Dutch Reformed Church set the stage for the March Federal Council Meeting.

The atmosphere was tense and politically charged as the top leaders of all the branches of the Dutch Reformed Church gathered to discern the meaning of the gospel in South Africa today. In response to the service in St. George's Cathedral, the white Dutch Reformed Church had just issued an attack against Allan Boesak and Desmond Tutu, denouncing them as taking a "wicked path,"questioning their role as church leaders, accusing them of personal and political ambitions, and blaming them for promoting "lawlessness and revolution."

The Dutch Reformed Church's attack was front-page news in both the Afrikaner and English papers, and, as has often been the pattern, set the climate and provided the theological rationale for subsequent government attacks on the same church leaders. At no time during the entire council meeting was any concern expressed by white Dutch Reformed Church members, either publicly or privately, about the threats against Allan Boesak and his family.

A long table separated the black delegates from the white. The black delegates had to walk out the first day before the whites agreed to deal with their agenda concerning the crisis in the country.

The discussion which finally ensued the next day was extraordinary. Most of the black church agenda items concerning the division of the church, the destabilization of neighboring African countries by the South African government, detentions, bannings, and the state of emergency never came up. The discussion never got that far.

The white Dutch Reformed Church delegates pointed to the "reforms" reflected in their church statements and in government policy. Some argued that the "ugly part" of apartheid should be removed but that "separate development" could be a positive policy.

Professor Johan Heyns, moderator of the Dutch Reformed Church, passionately proclaimed, "We are here as blood brothers in Jesus Christ!" A Dutch Reformed Church minister added, "It was never the intention of separate development to hurt anybody." The church had the right intention in choosing its path, he contended. "We are a privileged people because of having the gospel and our lifestyle. We wanted to help all peoples." That help wasn't "paternalism," he argued, but "guardianship." He claimed that this "privileged people" had "made provisions for the needs of people so they will be happy where they are and not put them all in one bunch." The man's obvious sincerity was even more alarming than his words.

Allan Boesak rose to give the closing argument for the black churches. He expressed gratitude for the clarity of the debate; the white Dutch Reformed Church had clearly described apartheid as "our policy." He continued, "The Dutch Reformed Church says we need more time. . . . We have no more time. You cannot defend the indefensible. There is no such thing as the 'nice face' and 'ugly face' of apartheid. Only people who have not suffered can speak of positive sides and good intentions."

The debate moved on to the issue of "status confessionis," the proclamation that apartheid is not just wrong but is a sin and a heresy and that opposition to it must have the theological status of a confession of faith. Here the debate became most intense.

Many argued that the heart of the gospel was at stake as well as the unity of the church. "Apartheid is a denial of the work of Christ on the cross, which was to bring us together," said delegates from the black churches. "It is a crisis of faith which

brings us to confession." A few white Christians who had left
the Dutch Reformed Church made anguished pleas to their fellow white Christians, seemingly to no avail.

The reason the white Dutch Reformed Church has been referred to as the "National Party at prayer" was quite apparent.
From helping to create apartheid at its inception, to justifying
its policies and laws at every stage of development, to now defending the government's current policy of "reform" without
real change, the Dutch Reformed Church has remained a con-
sistent supporter of the white South African government. The
Dutch Reformed Church has never dissented from government
policy nor ever defended the rights of those who are apartheid's
victims, even when they are brothers and sisters in Christ and
part of the same Reformed Church tradition.

Boesak looked across the room at his white colleagues and
said, "The time has come to call apartheid by its true name—a
sin—and to dismantle apartheid. The Dutch Reformed Church
must do it with the same energy as they used to establish apartheid, and we must help them. We understand the pain of the
Dutch Reformed Church in hearing these things. We don't enjoy
this. Is the Dutch Reformed Church willing to look its history
in the face? Is the Dutch Reformed Church willing to look its
victims in the face? Professor Heyns said today, 'We are blood
brothers.' I want to believe that with all my heart. But you don't
treat blood brothers the way you have treated us, the way you
have treated the people of South Africa. We keep coming back
to you again and again. We say this in love and charity, and we
will stay with you as long as we can."

The impassioned plea stirred the room. But the white delegates of the Dutch Reformed Church were able to derail a clear
vote on the heresy statement by manipulating both parliamen-
tary procedures and a call to prayer. The meeting ended for the
evening; many of the black church delegates elected not to return for the final day of meetings.

I went instead with Boesak to Johannesburg, where we met
with Frank Chikane, the general secretary of the South African
Council of Churches (SACC). Building on the foundations laid
by his predecessors, Desmond Tutu and Beyers Naudé, Chi-

kane's energetic and dynamic leadership has enabled the SACC to become the main vehicle through which the churches' resistance to apartheid is now being organized.

Most of the country's mainline churches are members of the SACC, even the Dutch Reformed Church branches, with the obvious exception of the white Dutch Reformed Church. The membership of these churches, like the population of the country, is 80 percent black, and in recent years the leadership has also become increasingly black. That new leadership, with the bold direction of people such as Chikane, Boesak, and Tutu, is creating a new climate in churches historically known for their passivity or occasional protest — but little real resistance — to apartheid.

Chikane was still talking about the surprising and exciting unity of the church leaders on the day of the Parliament March. The plan now was to mobilize the masses in the membership of the churches to join with their leaders in a new campaign of nonviolent resistance. Using the Parliament March as an example and tool, church-sponsored seminars on strategies for nonviolent resistance were being planned for local areas around the country. Chikane believes the church leaders have opened the door and legitimized the commitment to resistance. He firmly believes the congregations will follow.

The SACC has undertaken so many services and projects it has almost become an alternative government for the people of South Africa who have no government, but instead endure a state which is their predator. Hundreds of thousands of dollars are needed each month to support thousands of families of detainees. That assistance poses such a threat to the government that it continually seeks to undermine it. One such effort involved the creation of a counterfeit brochure by security police. Identical in format and typeface to an official SACC brochure, this version stated that the SACC support money goes toward "petrol bombs, tyres for necklaces, . . . condoms for AIDS, etc."

The government was also threatening to cut off, through legislation, crucial foreign financial support to the work of the SACC. Without that support the many relief and development projects supported by the SACC would be in great jeopardy.

The youth division of the SACC is deeply involved in the

black townships. The militant township youth, who provide so much energy to the struggle against apartheid, are finding new hope in the churches, mainly because of the leadership of people like Boesak and Tutu. Sometimes frustrated with the churches, many young people had drifted away, but the new role being undertaken by the church leaders has convinced many to not give up on the churches but instead to participate and criticize from within. In township after township we met young people who were excited about the arrests of church leaders on the Parliament March. We rarely found young people who felt the church to be irrelevant. Rather, many want the church to give them support and provide a strong base for their lives and their freedom struggle.

We joined in a special service at the SACC, offering thanksgiving for the stay of execution of the Sharpeville Six, who were to have been hanged that morning. Six young people had been given the death sentence for merely being part of a crowd that killed a local official. They were convicted under the law of "common purpose" and sentenced to death, though there was no proof they had anything to do with the violence of the rioting crowd. International pressure brought a temporary reprieve, and their sentences were later to be reduced to long prison terms.

During the service we sang a beautiful but sad song in Zulu, the words of which meant, "What have we done to deserve all this suffering? Our only sin is the color of our skin." We joined hands at the close of the service and sang "We Shall Overcome." One could feel the strength and suffering of a freedom struggle that transcends time and place and imagine how pleased Martin Luther King, Jr., would have been. The worshipers danced and sang their way out of the chapel, feet stomping, fingers pointed upward, and offering one last Zulu song whose words meant, "Don't let your heart be troubled. Do not worry. We have the victory."

A new attack on Desmond Tutu came in a letter from Botha [see pp. 144–47] which was carried widely in the newspapers. The state president was responding to the petition [see pp. 140–43] presented to the government on the day of the Parliament March. That petition, signed by the twenty-five church leaders, affirmed the "principles of nonviolent direct action," and said, in part:

> By imposing such drastic restrictions on organizations which have campaigned peacefully for the end of apartheid, you have removed nearly all effective means open to our people to work for true change by nonviolent means. . . . Your actions indicate to us that those of you in government have decided that only violence will keep you in power; that you have chosen the "military option" for our country. . . . We regard your restrictions not only as an attack on democratic activity in South Africa but as a blow directed at the heart of the church's mission in South Africa. The activities which have been prohibited are central to the proclamation of the Gospel in our country and we must make it clear that, no matter what the consequences, we will explore every possible avenue for continuing the activities which you have prohibited other bodies from undertaking. . . . We have not undertaken this action lightly. We have no desire to be martyrs. However, the Gospel leaves us no choice but to seek ways of witnessing effectively and clearly to the values of our Lord and Saviour Jesus Christ. . . .

In his letter Botha challenged:

> The question must be posed whether you are acting on behalf of the kingdom of God, or the kingdom promised by the ANC [African National Congress] and the SACP [South African Communist Party]? If it is the latter, say so, but do not then hide behind the structures and the cloth of the Christian church. . . . I wish to ask you whether it is not true . . . if [the church] brings its spiritual power into the secular power-play, and the message of Christ into disrepute, then it becomes a secular instead of a sacred spiritual subject, thereby relinquishing its claim to be church?

In East London, we stayed with a Dutch Reformed Mission Church pastor who had been detained. In South Africa, imprisonment is becoming an inevitable consequence of genuine Christian ministry. So many people have been to prison here, especially the young people. For young blacks, detention normally means beatings and torture as well.

There are so many stories—the child who didn't come back, the man detained over the weekend of his father's funeral, the wife who had to tell her detained husband that their baby died of malnutrition. They say that in Stalin's Russia, every family was touched by repression. That is true now of South Africa; virtually every black family is touched by detention, disappearance, police violence, injury, torture, or killing.

During a visit to Duncan Village, a black township near East London, we were detained and interrogated for about an hour. A young man who lives in the township and who was taking us around was picked up with us. Backed by soldiers and guns, a menacing security police officer threatened our twenty-four-year-old companion, who had recently been released from ten months of detention. He looked his intimidator in the eyes, pulled his New Testament out of his pocket, and courageously said, "I am a Christian."

We arrived back where we were staying in Buffalo Flats, a so-called colored area. The afternoon had been hot and tense, and I walked out on the little balcony behind the house to catch the cool breeze. I looked across the Buffalo River, over the huge ravine which separated us from the affluent white area of East London.

I could see the beautiful, white homes in the distance and wondered about the people who live there. How many have ever seen the black township of Duncan Village, from which we had just come? How many could even imagine it? How many would believe that the terrible poverty and repressive violence we just saw were true? Not very many, I was afraid.

How many even have questions and care enough to find out what's happening in their own country? If they would find out, and act, it would be costly to them. Perhaps that's what whites secretly know. The system works by offering whites a mixture of privilege and fear—all designed to sustain white ignorance.

Apartheid is designed to keep people separate. That part, at least, seems to be working.

The presence and power of evil is palpable here. You can feel it and it makes you shiver. Yet, alongside the power of the evil, one feels the vibrant hope of the people.

There is so much defiance and determination from so many. They are so young and so strong. It is a weak system that requires such overwhelming force to maintain itself. It is crumbling, from constant pressure and internal moral decay. The inevitability of the defeat of apartheid seems utterly clear.

I was called into the house. P. W. Botha was on television denouncing the church leaders. Frank Chikane, in his capacity as general secretary of the South African Council of Churches, had written Botha a letter which responded to the government's attack on Desmond Tutu and other church leaders. Chikane's letter (which, of course, wasn't reported by the South African press) said in part:

We feel that this unprecedented attack on the clergy may be paving the way for a state clampdown on the church and its witness to the truth. The church throughout the ages has borne the brunt of such attacks while governments have come and gone. We therefore pledge ourselves to the gospel of Christ against the forces of evil of this country and we commit ourselves to working for the ushering in of a new order of peace and justice for all; we make that pledge and commitment irrespective of the consequences. [See pp. 156–58 for the full text of the letter.]

Now Botha was on television in angry reply to Frank Chikane:

I grew up in an environment where the Lord was served, where the love of God, His Church, and His Word was transferred to me, and which I cherish in my heart to this very day. That is why I strive to conduct my personal life, and my service as State President, according to the principles of the Christian faith. This government has, in the light of the message of the Bible, gone out of its way to serve the people of this country. . . .

It is therefore disturbing that you and others, who claim to represent the Church of Christ and the Word of God,

act in the irresponsible way that you do. You do not hesitate to spread malicious untruths about South Africa here
and abroad. You should be fully aware of the numerous
misleading statements concerning local support for sanctions and for the ANC, alleged atrocities by the security
forces, the treatment of youths, and the fabrication of false
testimony for especially the overseas media. You love and
praise the ANC/SACP with its Marxist and atheistic ideology, land mines, bombs, and necklaces perpetrating the
most horrendous atrocities imaginable; and you embrace
and participate in their call for violence, hatred, sanctions,
insurrection, and revolution. . . .

It is alarming that God, and the Church of God which
I also love and serve, can be abused and insulted in this
manner; that individual members of the clergy, who claim
to be messengers of God, are in reality messengers of enmity and hatred while parading in the cloth, and hiding behind the structures of the Church. . . . In the name of God
and in the spirit of true Christianity I call upon you to be
messengers of the true Christian religion, and not of Marxism and atheism. . . .

It is a well-known fact that South Africa is a country
which cherishes and safeguards freedom of religion. . . .
Can you quote one single instance from the Word of God
in which it appears that Christ advocated violence against
the State; or led a demonstration against the State; or
broke a law of the State?

Immediately following Botha's attack was a special report by
the South African Broadcasting Corporation (SABC) on the
persecution of religion in the Soviet Union.

The next day was Palm Sunday, and I had been asked to
preach. A few hours after our incident in the township, a military
casspir (large armored personnel carrier) slowly drove past the
house where we were staying—a typical tactic of intimidation,
we were told. I was also warned that there would be police
informers in the congregation the next morning. That, too, is
common in South Africa. The text was how Jesus set his face

for Jerusalem, knowing what would be waiting for him there. We were about to enter Holy Week. I was struck with the realization that much of the South African church would not merely be remembering the momentous events of Holy Week but, in fact, living through them, in the midst of their own situation.

The next day's newspaper headlines in the Cape Town newspapers read "Boesak Fears Assassination." In his Palm Sunday sermon, Boesak told his congregation about all the threats, but challenged them to remain faithful and believe in God's promises. A special delegation from the World Alliance of Reformed Churches had come to offer international support for Allan and the embattled black Dutch Reformed Churches.

Earlier in the week, an Anglican delegation, including a representative of the Archbishop of Canterbury, had arrived to demonstrate worldwide Anglican solidarity with Archbishop Desmond Tutu. Meanwhile, Botha had gone on television to give his reply to possible legal action against him from the Anglicans for his attacks on Tutu. "I would like it! I would like it!" Botha shouted to a cheering crowd of white Afrikaners.

The same week *The New Nation* was banned for three months by the government. Sponsored by the Catholic Bishops Conference, this independent newspaper had been one of the last free voices among South Africa's heavily censored press and government-controlled media. During this Lent and Holy Week in South Africa, hardly a day went by without public confrontation between the church and the state.

Our Holy Week was spent mostly in townships and squatter camps around Cape Town. Crossroads, the squatter camp well known for its resistance, looks like a war zone now. The people there have suffered such violence for so long. Resistance to the government policy of forced removal is very high and very costly.

A theological student took us from one area to another, tracing the history of the government's efforts to move black people farther and farther from white areas. The Group Areas Act may be the most heartless and cruel policy of apartheid. We never met black people who were living where they were from—all had been removed by force from their homes.

Before the Group Areas Act, blacks, so-called coloreds, Indians, and even some whites lived together quite successfully. Now all that has changed.

Black people are always on the move in South Africa. There is no rest and there is no home. The pain of just seeing it is almost too much to bear. To experience it would be much worse. As we saw, heard, and felt the sheer weight of human suffering caused by this diabolical system, the words rose up from my soul: "Apartheid was conceived in hell."

A Holy Week strategy session at Bishopscourt at the residence of Archbishop Tutu brought together twenty-five people. The discussion soon focused on whether the churches were ready to follow their leaders into serious nonviolent resistance. Theologian Charles Villa-Vicencio pointed out how domesticated many in the churches still are and that, while a church-state conflict was escalating, there was still a real struggle ahead within the churches.

Most agreed, however, that the churches were ready as never before and the government would not succeed in isolating the church leaders. The time to act was now, and next steps were planned to take the issues into the heart of the churches while publicly confronting the government's policies. The "campaign," as people referred to it, was everywhere gaining momentum since the Parliament March and would now be carried to regional and local levels.

On Wednesday, on the way to Lavendar Hill, we passed a school with all of the children being held outside and surrounded by a large group of police. Such sights are very familiar in South Africa.

In Lavendar Hill, we met Jan de Waal, who helped start a community center there in one of the most overcrowded townships. A conversation ensued about white South Africa. De Waal spoke of the tremendous indoctrination whites are subjected to. If whites choose to join in the anti-apartheid struggle, they experience tremendous rejection from their own community, friends, and even family. Virtually all the whites we met who were seriously involved told us the same thing.

Beyers Naudé, South Africa's best-known white dissident, told us later in Johannesburg that he was not optimistic about white involvement. "You must be willing to risk your income, your security, and your very life. You have to be prepared to be ostracized by your own people and walk by faith with God. Until they come to that point, whites will be unwilling."

"The difference between liberals and radicals," said de Waal, "is more than analysis. It's the difference of involvement." Whites involved in the struggle live as foreigners in their white areas, with almost all their social contact in the black community. Jan de Waal's own involvement has, among other things, cost him sight in his right eye as a result of being struck by a police baton during a protest march.

At the New World Center in Lavender Hill, the church is used for everything—morning day care, community noon meal, after-school programs, evening church activities, Sunday church, and meetings dealing with community and political issues. It was a stark contrast to the beautiful, stately, and usually locked Dutch Reformed churches we saw everywhere we went in South Africa.

The truth about South Africa was dramatically brought home to me on the outskirts of Lavender Hill, at the juxtaposition of a wretched squatter camp and an incredibly opulent white area just two minutes away. Rather than being an ugly aberration, South Africa is really an extreme parable of an entire global system.

It is literally the First World and the Third World living side by side in the closest proximity—with the one literally killing the other for the sake of its own wealth and privilege, and the other suffering and dying, just out of the sight and hearing of most of its executioners. This bleeding land is a microcosm of the oppressive dynamics which now govern the world order.

On Easter Sunday, April 3, Allan Boesak preached to the memory of Martin Luther King, Jr., who died twenty years earlier on April 4. He spoke passionately about what the martyred American prophet meant to him and to South Africa. King is everywhere around Allan Boesak—his home and office are full of pictures, books, tapes, and mementos. Boesak is self-consciously a disciple of King and makes regular reference to him and the freedom movement he led. Now more than ever, Allan Boesak and other South African church leaders are reflecting on King and the relevance of his radical nonviolence for the next phase of South Africa's history.

Later in Easter week, we met with Nico Smith in his home in Mamelodi, a township outside Pretoria. Like Beyers Naudé, Smith left the white Dutch Reformed Church to join the black church; he is one of the very few whites who have chosen to live in a black township.

"The greatest problem in our country," said Smith, "is that too many people have accepted Christ—the 'mystical Christ,' the Christ of personal experiences and inner emotions. Seventy-five percent of the white people accept the mystical Christ, and in the meantime, the devil is lord of the country and in their lives, too."

The false gospel preached by the white South African churches "immunizes people to the real gospel," he explained. "When you put the false gospel into their veins and minds, they resist the real gospel. When they hear the real thing, they believe it is dangerous and they must fight it."

Whites can't believe or understand what's happening in their country, Smith said. "When they say, 'I don't believe it,' it's another way of saying, 'I don't understand it,' which is another way of saying, 'I don't know about it,' which is a way of saying, 'I'm not responsible for it.' "

Few whites have taken responsibility—or given up their privilege. A youth in Mamelodi told us, "The whites don't believe in our 'one man, one vote.' They believe in 'one man, one pool'—and they use their vote to keep their pool."

We spent a day in Soweto with Frank Chikane and his family. Their house had been petrol-bombed in 1985.

Chikane had a conservative evangelical upbringing, similar to my own. We reflected on the times the strength of such a history can be drawn upon, especially when in jail. His humbly told story of how detentions, torture, and an underground existence ultimately led to his appointment as general secretary of the South African Council of Churches (while he was still in hiding from the government) was a moving testimony of faith in the promises of God.

He took us around Soweto, the black township of two million

people that is actually larger than neighboring Johannesburg. Soweto is an awesome spectacle of humanity: groaning under the pain of the present but pulsing with the hope of South Africa's future. We went back to Soweto often.

One incident in Soweto will remain with me for a long time. We were in Soweto for a detainees' support meeting. The large hall was jammed—packed with people from the township, especially those who had been detained and the families of detainees. A militant spirit soon took over as the young people made it their meeting with their chants, fiery speeches, and freedom songs.

Thirty thousand people had been detained since the state of emergency was imposed on June 12, 1986—ten thousand of them under the age of sixteen. Add to that the assassinations, disappearances, random killings, little children shot down in the streets, and no one brought to justice for any of these crimes— what else but the cross could bear the overwhelming weight of such suffering and pain?

Near the end of the support meeting, all eyes focused on a group of children about to perform on the stage. Some were no older than eight or nine, the oldest about fourteen. They were very good as they acted out little vignettes of township life— some humorous, some serious, and all very militant.

The concluding dramatization was the longest and most substantial. It opened with a scene of township unrest and the painful sight of a black policeman brutalizing black people. The crowd booed.

The second scene took place at night. In shadows, the black policeman came to the door of one whom he had brutalized. "Please, I've fallen out of favor with my white superiors. I have nowhere to go. Will you take me in? Can you forgive me?"

"Forgive you!" replied the man at the door. "Only God could forgive you! I will not. Now get away from my house!" He slammed the door.

As he moved back into his home, he began to talk to himself: "But wait, Jesus tells us that we must turn the other cheek and forgive those who persecute us, even our enemies. . . . I must go to him."

When the man came out of his house into the street he saw

that some township young people had found the police traitor and were about to "necklace" him by lighting a gasoline-filled tire around his neck. The man jumped in between the youth and the policeman. "No wait! We must not do this! Yes, this man has been an instrument of our oppression, but also of his own. Jesus tells us to forgive those who persecute us. We must forgive him because he is really our brother. He must be welcomed back and restored to us again. He can join with us in the struggle." The man said, "I was so stupid to be used by the whites as an instrument to kill my nation." They released him.

The next scene was one of protest. All were in the street with placards. Among them was the former policeman. The riot police opened fire—the forgiven policeman was hit and lay dying in the arms of his comrades. "I never knew the liberation struggle until I joined it," he said. "I never knew a bullet until I felt it in my flesh."

In the final scene, they buried their long-lost and new-found brother. At the funeral they knelt and they stood, heads bowed and hands raised offering prayers for Africa. "Lord, we are tired of bullets," they prayed. "Please give us peace and freedom." They ended with the Lord's Prayer.

Tears came to my eyes. The audience was quiet and then slowly began to clap, to cheer, and then to sing freedom songs. "God bless Africa," they sang.

If white South Africa rejects this revolution, I thought to myself, it may be the last chance it will ever have. This revolution is not just the church leaders, it's a nation, and a people, and a movement whose faith reaches right down to the grassroots. That faith is now being rediscovered at a critical moment of South Africa's history. The seeds of radical Christian faithfulness sown by a courageous minority over many years may now finally be ready to bear much fruit. But the cost of faithfulness will be high.

The South African government banned democratic peaceful protest and has proven that it really wants violent confrontation. The military option is the natural preference for a regime whose only legitimacy is the power of the gun. It is into that political vacuum and crucible of fire that the churches are deciding to walk, and they are choosing the path of nonviolent resistance.

During the last few days of May 1988, the South African Council of Churches convened a convocation of more than two hundred church leaders. The group voted to launch a new campaign of nonviolent action to remove the system of apartheid. That decision continued a series of momentous events which began with the Parliament March on February 29 and which together signify a new day for the church and a new stage in the South African freedom struggle.

The church is becoming the church in South Africa. The process of "becoming" is never easy, and this is no exception. The May convocation showed that there are still differences among church leaders regarding perspective, pace, and preferred strategies, and these need to be overcome. But there is more unity than ever before.

The choice between negotiation and confrontation is now clearly in the government's hands. Black leaders have always been willing to negotiate if the white government is prepared to discuss real change, but so far, negotiation has been a smokescreen for a surrender to white power.

The intransigence of the white South African government, the suffering endured by the people, and the momentum of the situation make more confrontation inevitable. What kind of confrontation there will be and what kind of new South Africa will emerge are the real questions now. In finding answers to these questions, the role of the South African churches will be absolutely crucial.

The white government's policy to destroy all dissent has not been effective. The military predominates as an overwhelming steamroller that seeks to crush every challenge to white control. Against such enormous power, creativity and courage will be the most needed characteristics of any opposition.

To fight the apartheid regime on its own terms is to court disaster. The ever-present temptation to submit to despair and revenge can lead only to certain defeat. Mere rhetoric and constant reaction will be no substitute for clear strategy and fresh initiatives.

The power of nonviolent resistance to mobilize moral authority, popular participation, and the human resources of the majority could open up new possibilities at a most critical time. It is apparent that many South African Christians are counting the cost of such a commitment.

During times of protest, candles are lit in windows to show solidarity and hope; and the police come into people's homes to blow the candles out. The children make jokes about the South African government being afraid of candles.

On our first day in South Africa, in St. George's Cathedral, Desmond Tutu began his sermon, "In the enveloping darkness — as the lights of freedom are extinguished one by one — despite all the evidence to the contrary, we have come here to say that evil, and injustice, and oppression, and exploitation — embodied in the very essence, the very nature of apartheid — cannot prevail."

Forty days later, after witnessing the power of the church all over South Africa, I believed more than ever the words from John's Gospel: "The light shines in the darkness, and the darkness has not overcome it."

In February 1988, church leaders march on parliament to protest banning of anti-apartheid organizations: Archbishop Stephen Naidoo, Archbishop Desmond Tutu (Roman Catholic and Anglican Archbishops of Cape Town), Allan Boesak, and Frank Chikane. All were arrested.

Allan Boesak (right) and Desmond Tutu at special service at St. George's Cathedral in Cape Town. The service was called to protest restrictions on anti-apartheid organizations: "No government can challenge the living God and survive."

2

Your Days Are Over!

A Sermon by Allan Boesak

---

*Like the sermon by Desmond Tutu (see pp. 33–39), this ser-
mon was delivered in St. George's Cathedral, Cape Town, on
March 13, 1988, at a Prayer Service for Justice and Liberation
in South Africa. Allan Boesak is the president of the World
Alliance of Reformed Churches.*

My dear brothers and sisters, I would like to read to you a
few verses from the first book of Kings, chapter 19, upon which
what I have to say to you today will be based:

> Ahab told Jezebel all that Elijah had done, and how he
> had slain all the prophets with a sword. Then Jezebel sent
> a messenger to Elijah, saying, "So may the Gods do to me
> and more also, if I do not make your life as the life of one
> of them by this time tomorrow." Elijah was afraid, and he
> arose and went for his life, and came to Beersheba, which
> belongs to Judah, and left his servant there. But he himself
> went a day's journey into the wilderness and came and sat
> down under a broom tree; and he asked that he might die,
> saying, "It is enough, now, O Lord, take away my life; for
> I am no better than my fathers."

And then again we read from that same chapter that the Lord
asked Elijah, "What are you doing here, Elijah?" This is after

Elijah had left and gone to Horeb, the mountain of God.

Elijah said, "I have been very zealous for the Lord, the God of hosts; for the people of Israel have forsaken thy covenant, thrown down thine altars, and slain thy prophets with a sword. And I, even I alone, am left; and they seek my life to take it away."

"Yet," God said, "I will leave seven thousand in Israel—all the knees that have not bowed to Baal, and every mouth that has not kissed him."

I thought, my brothers and sisters, it would be important for us to talk a little bit about this portion of scripture today. It's so well known to those of us who read our Bibles regularly—and who go to church regularly and do not waste our time thinking of new laws and therefore being left with no time to go to church on Sunday morning.

It's a very beautiful story, one of those gripping stories that I remember from my childhood so well. Elijah—that great prophet who becomes the symbol of prophecy for Israel and for the church of all times—now under this broom tree completely dispirited, tired, ready even to give up his life.

It's a little strange, though; because you will remember just before that, in 1 Kings chapter 18, there was this marvelous event where Elijah had made up his mind that now is the time to come to grips with Israel, and with all these prophets of Baal who were misleading the people, and with Jezebel and her husband, Ahab, who formed the government of the day.

So they came to Mount Carmel, and there Elijah made his challenge: "Today you must make your choice. Either you choose Baal, or you choose God. And don't sit here and worry, what shall I do? what shall I not do? Make your choice today very clear."

You will remember also the incredible victory for Elijah and for God on that day. It must have felt very, very good after all of that.

And then came the message from Jezebel, saying, "Tomorrow I will have you killed, because you are the kind of minister who does not want to keep out of politics." That's essentially what she said. "You keep on interfering, you are inspired by I don't know who. But I am telling you now, you must stop this, because you are going to die."

Then strangely, or maybe not so strangely, Elijah flees for his life, finds himself under this broom tree, and says to God, "It is over now, God. I cannot take this anymore. I cannot stand all these threats anymore. I cannot fight this battle anymore. I am just a normal, simple human being. I am no better than my fathers. I am not some superman. I am just a human being, and I cannot take this anymore!"

And then there comes this marvelous moment where God sends the angel, and the angel tells Elijah, "Rise up and eat; otherwise the journey will be too much for you, because I want you to go on even further than you have come now."

We mostly stop reading there. And then we say, "Isn't it marvelous? Elijah is tired, and God comes and gives him sustenance for the road ahead, and everything from now on is going to be hunky-dory."

But that's not true. The story does not end there, because God says, "There is still a journey ahead of you."

And we might ask, "What journey?" because Elijah had no intention to go on another journey. He wanted to die there, remember? He had no intention to go on another journey. He did not have the courage to face Jezebel and Ahab again. He did not want to go on with his life, because he thought it did not matter anymore: "I'm going to die anyway, and the powers of this world are far too powerful. I am just a small person. I cannot take this anymore."

He had no intention of going anywhere, although God said, "Oh no, Elijah. This is not the end of the road for you. There is still some work for you to do. You have a journey ahead of you."

And so he goes along this road to Mount Horeb itself, the mountain of God. And then it says he comes to this cave, where he has this wonderful experience of God revealing himself to Elijah.

Now we must not read over those words as if they were just printed there. That is the same mountain where Moses went. And when Moses said to God, "How can I go forward with these people if things are like this? What is the future of Israel? What

have we done and what will we do if you will not go with us?"
God says, "Go and stand at the mouth of the cave"—the same
cave where Elijah now finds himself. There he experienced
something of the glory of God.

Go back and read that story. It says then that Elijah saw a
fire; but God was not in the fire. There was a strong wind; but
God was not in the wind. There came the earthquake; and God
was not in the earthquake. And then there came a strange, quiet
stillness. A silence. And God was in the silence.

Let's talk a little bit about that. I am preaching to you today.
Last time when we met somewhere else, I was making a speech.
I want to preach to you today—it's Sunday, and I want you to
understand. And I want [Minister of Law and Order Adriaan]
Vlok and all those people who never go to church to understand.
(Hopefully they'll steal some of these TV tapes again like they
usually do; they've stopped listening to us, but maybe they'll be
forced to look at each other if they hear the word of God.)

So here you have Elijah, this prophet of God, who was ready
to give up and not to fight anymore. And then there comes a
question. Three times God says, "What are you doing here,
Elijah?"

Now some of these clever theologians, the professors, said in
the seminary, that this is a question of reproach. "What are you
doing here, Elijah?" They think God is saying, "You ought to
be out there on the battlefield. You ought to be out there confronting Jezebel. You ought to be confronting Ahab. You ought
to be out there getting God's people together and fighting the
good fight with all your might," and so forth. "That is what you
are supposed to be doing! What are you doing here on this
mountain?"

But I don't believe that that is true. I don't think that the
question that God is putting to Elijah is a question of reproach.
I think, rather, my brothers and sisters, it is a question of understanding. God understands that there may come a time in
the life of people when we get tired. God understands that the
struggle is a long, drawn-out, painful, tear-filled struggle, and
we may get tired. God understands that the powers that we face
in this world are the powers of evil, and destruction, and violence, and intimidation, and we get tired. God understands that

you cannot stand on your toes all the time every day.

God understands that when you get up in the morning and you have to fight the same fight that you have been fighting for twenty years and forty years and fifty years—God knows that you get tired. That little sticker that says, "Ten years of P. W. Botha, and forty years of apartheid, and a lifetime of suffering" is so true. God understands that.

And so our battle has come. For over three hundred years now we have been fighting for our human dignity, and we get tired. We have been fighting for liberation and for freedom, and sometimes we get tired. We have been fighting against this government that has done everything in its power to cripple our movement and to kill off our people, and we get tired. It's true, and we might as well admit it.

I admit to you that sometimes I get tired of fighting the same battle over and over again. Two years of a state of emergency, children of eight and nine and ten and eleven and twelve years old in prison being tortured, children being shot in the streets, parents not knowing where to go, our hearts filled with despair day after day after day. Sometimes, sometimes you get tired.

Sometimes we get tired of picking up the telephone and wondering whether there's going to be another threat against our lives. We get tired of wondering, when will the vilification end? When will they stop trying to subject us to the kind of psychological and physical terror that our people have been living under? And so sometimes, just sometimes, we feel like Elijah.

But you must not worry when you feel like that, my brothers and sisters. Don't feel bad, because God understands. Don't think that God wants you to be strong all the time, twenty-four hours a day, sixty minutes of every hour, sixty seconds of every minute. God understands.

God understands, because Elijah was in that same position, and God told Elijah, "I understand, Elijah, just how you feel. I understand your pain. I understand the worry that you carry in your heart. I understand what it is that makes you so concerned."

But God also says, "Don't lie there, Elijah. Even though I understand, don't give up now. Get up there and walk to the mountain of God, because I have a message for you. I have work for you."

When Elijah comes there and meets with God, and God appears to Elijah, that voice in the stillness says two things. One, it says, "Don't give up now, you've got to go on, because I have work for you to do." And secondly the voice says, "There are still seven thousand who have not bowed the knee to Baal."

What must Elijah go and do? If you finish chapter 19, then you've got to go on to chapter 20, and 21, and 22, and then you'll find out that God says to Elijah, "Go and tell Ahab, 'Ahab, you have displeased me. I am going to take away from you your kingship. You will no longer sit on the throne of Israel.' Go and tell Jezebel, 'The dogs will eat your flesh.' " That is the kind of work that Elijah has to do for God.

My brothers and sisters, think of what is happening in this country; think of how time after time after time we have to try again — and you try again, and the church meetings get banned, and our own rallies get banned, and churches get tear-gassed, and people get detained, and children get terrorized.

But don't give up the struggle now. Don't say, "Let us lie down under the broom tree." Don't say, "There is nothing more for us to do." Don't say, "There is no future for us." Don't say, "There is no road for us to walk on." Because God has work for you to do. And Bishop [Tutu], you and I have to do the work of Elijah. We will have to go to this Jezebel who sits in Pretoria; you and I will have to go to P. W. Ahab, and we will have to say to him — it's true, just listen — the same message that Elijah was giving to Ahab and Jezebel: "Your days are over! God has decided you will no longer sit on the throne of Israel. You shall die in the face of this God!"

It's the same message that the church today is called to go and give to the Ahabs and Jezebels of this land and our day. We must tell P. W. Botha, "We have stood up from under the broom tree. We are sick enough; we are exhausted; and through our tiredness and our tears, we have been given courage by this God who never leaves his people alone. And we will tell you your days are over! You can forget it, your days are over!"

It doesn't matter whether they ban us. It doesn't matter whether they threaten us. It doesn't matter whether they throw us in jail. It doesn't matter whether they tell us that we have been inspired by I don't know who.

The point that they must hear, and hear very clearly, is that the church in South Africa has decided we have work to do in this country. We shall continue to do that work until freedom comes for our people and the demands of God's justice are being met in South Africa.

And so we may be tired today, but we will go on, for we have work to do. As long as apartheid exists, we have work to do. As long as our people are detained, we have work to do. As long as the church and our people are being threatened, we have work to do. As long as there is a [government] minister who thinks that he's God, we have work to do.

I just came back from Johannesburg, and on the plane some person gives me this newspaper. In the newspaper it says, "Vlok tells churchmen: Toe the line, or else." I don't want to defy Adriaan Vlok. I don't even want to argue with Adriaan Vlok, because it is not worth it. That is not my point. My point is not that I want to challenge this man. I just want to say to him, "Adriaan Vlok, who do you think you are?"

Where does he get the arrogance to tell the church of God we must toe the line? Whose line must the church toe in South Africa? There is only one line that we toe, and that's God's line!

I don't want to challenge the minister. I don't want to argue with the minister. I don't want to do anything with this man. I just want to tell him, "You can forget about threatening the church of Jesus Christ."

You know, the problem with Adriaan Vlok and P. W. Botha and all these people is that they think that they are talking to Desmond Tutu and Allan Boesak. They will live to regret that mistake! They are not talking to Allan Boesak, they are not talking to Desmond Tutu, they're not talking to any of us. They are actually taking on God himself, and they will regret it!

The Minister of Law and Order says that we must speak to the Christian message. Isn't that the problem—when you belong to a church that has, for so many years, distorted the Christian message to such an extent that no one in that church recognizes the truth anymore? That is the problem when you are a member of a church that calls itself Reformed but has denied every basic tenet of the Reformed tradition. That is the problem when you belong to a church that does not have the courage and the guts to teach its people what justice and peace mean today in South Africa, because it is a church that is tied hand and foot to the status quo and to the continuation of apartheid and of injustice in South Africa.

If his church had taught him, the minister would have known what the Christian message is. But, you see, he does not. And so he says, "Speak to the Christian message." Well, Mr. Minister, let me say again—if you had read the Gospels, if your church had taught you, you would not have spoken such utter nonsense.

To feed the poor and clothe the naked is the Christian message. To fight for justice *is* the Christian message. To say that peace without justice is impossible in South Africa, as anywhere else in the world, is the Christian message. To say that a government which knows no justice and denies God is illegitimate and will die ignominiously is the Christian message. To proclaim to this government, that in your denial of the word of God, in your insistence upon oppression, in your persecution of the church of Jesus Christ, you have ceased to become the servant of God of Romans 13 but you have become the beast from the sea of Revelation 13—that is the Christian message that the government must hear. To call upon God's people to obey God rather than the government *is* the Christian message. So we say to the government, "Mr. Vlok, you know, you can do with us whatever you want any day." It's true. That man can kill us in the streets and nothing will happen to him, he thinks. But it does not matter in the end. He is destined to hear the word of God from the church of Jesus Christ in South Africa.

I call upon the church, my brothers and my sisters. We are entering now a new phase of persecution of the church in this country. But there can be no turning back. Those of you who have decided to follow Jesus Christ must follow Jesus Christ now, even into the streets of this country and into the face of the casspirs [armored personnel carriers], and the guns, and the water cannons, and the tear gas. Those of you who have decided to follow Jesus Christ, don't turn back now because this monster has reared its ugly head once again. That is not what we are here for. What you have to understand is that the church's witness in this country today will stand or fall by our faithfulness in confronting the South African government and the evil it persists in doing.

When the law is passed that stops the church from getting funds from abroad, they will say other churches in the world have no right to support the church in South Africa because our activities are subversive. That will be another challenge for the church, because the issue is not whether we get money or not. The issue that is at stake will be whether the church in South Africa will allow the government—a secular institution, a non-Christian body—to tell the church what church work is, or to tell the church what the gospel says it must do, or to tell the church where we can do the work of the church.

The government must understand and the church must understand: There is no question that the church cannot allow the South African government to dictate to it what the mission of the church is in South Africa. When they stop the money, the church will have to say, "We will go and get that money." We will bring that money in and let them throw us in jail again, because it is the mission of the church to serve the poor, the weak, the naked, and the oppressed, and the South African government has no right to stop us.

Amidst all of the warnings that we get these days, we have to proclaim one thing, and this is that Jesus Christ is Lord. I know how difficult it sometimes may be. I know how I felt on that Thursday night when that brick flew through our window, fortunately without hurting any of our children. But it must be said: Jesus Christ is Lord. I want to say this as calmly as I possibly can. Mr. Minister, you can threaten us all you like—Jesus Christ is Lord. You can put us in jail as many times as you like—Jesus Christ is Lord. Let your security police terrorize our children and threaten our lives—Jesus Christ is Lord. You can come into the streets and into our churches and you can massacre us—Jesus Christ is Lord. The battle is on! But Jesus Christ is Lord.

And so the government of South Africa has signed its own death warrant. No government can challenge the living God and survive. And that, Mr. Minister, is the good news for the people of God and the bad news for you.

Desmond Tutu at the service at St. George's Cathedral: "Freedom is coming, because that is God's will for us."

3

Clarifying the Word

A Sermon by Desmond Tutu

Desmond Tutu, Anglican archbishop of Cape Town, gave the following sermon on March 13, 1988, in St. George's Cathedral, Cape Town. The sermon was given at a Prayer Service for Justice and Liberation in South Africa. The service was held in response to the government's banning of the Committee to Defend Democracy, which had been formed only days before by a group of church leaders in protest of the government's recent assault on democratic groups.

We are gathered today to pray for our country facing a deepening crisis, to reflect on what is taking place, and our role as believers—as Christians, as Muslims, as Jews, whatever. What would be our role in this crisis? In the enveloping darkness—as the lights of freedom are extinguished one by one—despite all the evidence to the contrary, we have come here to say that evil, and injustice, and oppression, and exploitation—embodied in the very essence, the very nature, of apartheid—cannot prevail.

In the Bible, we are told to speak to spiritual things. St. John says, "The light shineth in the darkness, and the darkness did not overwhelm the light." We come to sustain our hope that this is so. Humanly speaking, as we look around at our situation, that situation appears hopeless. But we must assert, and assert confidently, that this is God's world, that God is in charge.

We must say to our rulers, especially unjust rulers such as those in this land, "You may be powerful, indeed, very powerful. But you are not God. You are ordinary mortals! God—the God whom we worship—can't be mocked. You have already lost. You have already lost! Let us say to you nicely, 'You have already lost.' We are inviting you to come and join the winning side. Come! Come and join the winning side. Your cause is unjust. You are defending what is fundamentally indefensible, because it is evil. It is evil without question. It is immoral. It is immoral without question. It is un-Christian. Therefore, you will bite the dust! And you will bite the dust comprehensively!"

Now, in this land we have prostituted language, making words mean something other than their original meaning. I have written a new dictionary to help people understand how we use language in South Africa.

Now, you know the meaning of "voluntarily," don't you? "Voluntarily." You came to this service voluntarily. Nobody pushed you. You came because you wanted to come.

Now, look at the way we use language in this country. The government says the squatters are moving. How did they move? The government tells us they moved "voluntarily." In order to help them move "voluntarily," there are police around pointing guns.

The minister of law and order, in restricting the activities of a new committee, said he was doing so for the sake of "public safety." Now, you've got to be careful in this country. Do you remember Pavlov and his dog? Pavlov carried out experiments. He showed a dog meat, and the dog salivated when he saw the meat. Next he showed the dog meat and rang a bell. The dog salivated. He showed him meat, and then he rang a bell, and the dog again salivated. He showed him meat, and rang the bell, and the dog once again salivated. Then he took away the meat and simply rang the bell. The dog salivated. He called this a conditioned reflex.

Now, in this country, we have what are called conditioned reflexes. When the government uses certain words, they know that many people will react in the kind of way that they have conditioned people to react. So they say "public safety." Do you know what "public safety" means? "Public safety" means you can walk safely in public. The police exist to ensure that you can walk. Ha, ha!

What happens in this country? People say we want to protest peacefully against pass laws. The police ought to be around to see that those people have "public safety." But what do the police do? They shoot the people protesting peacefully. The protesters don't even have stones! Most of the sixty-nine killed at Sharpeville were shot in the back. They were shot in the back running away, shot by those who claim to be custodians of "public safety." We have never shot anyone. Has Allan Boesak ever shot anybody? Has the rector of the University of the Western Cape thrown a stone at anybody?

I don't know anything about formal law, but we have heard policemen confess that they beat people who are in their custody. "Public safety!" This committee [the Committee to Defend Democracy] has not done anything to undermine "public safety." We were not around when police went into a tirade. I'm not talking about something that they can disclaim. The inquest magistrate has said, "The police behaved irresponsibly." That's a mild term. They want the children to stone them, and when the children do something like that, they come out like cowboys with their guns blazing. They openly kill our children. "Public safety?" "Public safety."

This committee did not throw stones through office windows. We didn't throw stones through the windows of Allan Boesak's office. We didn't throw stones at the home of Allan Boesak. Who killed [Steve] Biko? Why is it that not one person has been apprehended and tried for those dastardly acts? "Public Safety" indeed. The greatest threat to "public safety" in South Africa is this government.

Then they say, "It is also in order to maintain public order." Now—we must say it clearly—all of us are law abiding. We obey the laws, because we know that any society, in order to survive, needs the structure of good law. If we all drove on any side of the road, chaos would result; eventually people would fall victim. We obey traffic laws which say you must travel on the left-hand side of the road.

And rulers, according to public order, cannot be arbitrary in the exercise of their power. For their power is not absolute.

Their power is regulated. Law must, as far as possible, embody morality.

South Africa is the only country in which it is a crime for a woman to sleep with her husband if her husband happens to be a migrant worker and she has not received permission to be where he is. That is the law. And to break that law is to do something that is illegal. But that law is fundamentally immoral; to obey it is to be guilty of immorality.

So, my friends, you must learn the difference between morality and legality. When something is legal, almost all of the people in the country think that it is also morally right. But it is not always so.

You are concerned for peace and stability when you are concerned for "public order." But what does the government of this country do? They tell protesters to "leave and don't ever come back again or be involved in these activities." What activities? Peacemaking activities? Crazy, crazy country! We stand things upside down in this country.

People ask [United Democratic Front co-president] Mrs. Albertina Sisulu, "Please Mrs. Sisulu, come and help us" whenever there is trouble. She leaves all her work and her children—those of them who are not in detention—and she comes here. She works like crazy. She works very hard. She knows the price for working for peace! Working for peace! She didn't come to make political speeches and to join the UDF. She comes saying, "Why can't you people unite?" The government then declares, "We restrict you for being involved in peacemaking."

Justice is blindfolded because justice must be evenhanded. Ha, ha! Evenhanded! The conservative Afrikaners walk in uniforms. And they look like Nazis. They've got a thing on their uniforms that looks like a swastika. And they shout anti-black slogans. They march against you. They march to the Union Center, and when they get there, do you think they get water-cannoned? I don't. The policemen there shake hands with them.

The only things we had in our hands [during the February 29, 1988, March to Parliament] were our Bibles. You know, this government is not quite as stupid as we think. We know how explosive the Bible is. We came along carrying Bibles.

Didn't we say long ago that apartheid is as evil as Nazism?

We said that long ago. And they said, "That Tutu character and all those others, they like to exaggerate. They are melodramatic."

Now you see that they can take action against people who are dressed like priests! We had nothing. We just linked our hands and we tried to pray. In fact, at the police station we said, "We would like to pray." A policeman replied, "This is a police station. You don't pray here."

Another word they like to use is "revolution." Revolution! They think we run away from revolution, but the people in this country do not think revolution is necessarily a bad thing. Revolution means a radical change. If it is revolutionary to say that I work for a South Africa that is nonracial; if it is revolutionary to say I am working for a South Africa that is truly democratic; if it is revolutionary to say I am working for a South Africa where black and white and yellow and green can work together arm-in-arm; then friends, I am for that!

I am willing to say to [Minister of Law and Order] Mr. Adriaan Vlok that I am going to continue saying the things that I have said and am saying today. Mr. Vlok, you have got all the laws that you can use if you want to use them. But I am not going to be told by you what the gospel of our Lord and Savior Jesus Christ must be. If preaching the gospel of Jesus Christ is going to lead me into any kind of trouble with you and your sort, tough luck! Tough luck.

I do not, in fact, know what the ANC [African National Congress] has said. But let me say it firmly—the ANC, the PAC [Pan African Congress], our organizations were legal until they were banned. They were operating above board and they were working nonviolently. And this government banned them.

I want to say, I am not a politician. I do not belong to political organizations. But I am not going to allow this government or any other government to choose my friends for me. If my friends happen to be in the ANC, I am not going to renounce them for that reason.

I have said—and let me say it yet again—I support the ANC in its objective for a new South Africa! That is not anything new. I said it, in fact, in the Supreme Court on one occasion, when I was arguing for litigation. I said to the judge, "I support the

ANC. And I support every organization that seeks a new kind of South Africa." I said, "I don't support the methods that they are using. But I stick to them. They are my brothers; they are my sisters; they are my friends; they are my fathers; they are my mothers. How can I repudiate them?"

The government once asked me to repudiate the ANC. I said,"OK. Will you, asking me that question, repudiate the fore-fathers? For, according to the laws of this country, they too would be guilty of terrorism. For they fought for their freedom. Why must it be OK when they fight for their freedom and when we do, it's not good?"

I do not get my mandate from any group. I get my mandate from the Bible. Our Lord and Savior Jesus Christ says, "The Spirit of the Lord has anointed me that I should preach good news to the poor, and freedom to those who are in prison, for the setting free of those who are enslaved." I didn't get that from a political charter. I got it from the Holy Bible, which they [whites] brought for us, and which we are taking seriously.

I finish, my friends, by saying—if they want to take on the church of God, I warn them. Read a little bit of history, and see what happened to those who tried to take on the church of God. Don't read all history. Just read your own history. I just warn them that even if they were to remove this, that, or the other person, the church of God will stay. Our Lord and Savior said, "Even the gates of hell will not prevail against the church of God."

And so we say, freedom is coming! Freedom is coming, be-cause that is God's will for us. Freedom is coming, because God did not make us doormats on which people can wipe their dirty boots. Freedom is coming, because God has created us for free-dom.

Freedom is coming. And we can all walk hand-in-hand, black and white, together. Proudly, holding our heads high in a new South Africa. A free South Africa. A South Africa where people count, because they are created in the image of God. A free South Africa where all of God's people will share equally the good things that God has given us.

Freedom is coming, and we want it also for you, Mr. Vlok. We want you to be able to sleep at night and not wonder what we are up to. We want you to sleep, Mr. Vlok, and not wonder, "Where is the UDF? Where is Boesak now? What is he doing?"

Freedom is coming even for you, Mr. P. W. Botha. We want you to be free. We want you to be here with us. We want you to put away the casspirs [armored personnel carriers]. Those chaps ought to be with their wives and children this afternoon.

Freedom is coming for all of us. There can be no doubt about it—because if God be for us, who can be against us?

Amen, and amen.

"What is a greater joy than to work for justice, to seek peace, to stand up for things that are worthwhile? To plead for the fatherless, the widow, and the poor, to take up their cause and fight for it, and to work for the realization of the kingdom of God. What is greater joy than that?"

4

At the Apocalypse: The South African Church Claims Its Hope

An Interview with Allan Boesak

Allan Boesak, president of the World Alliance of Reformed Churches and moderator of the Dutch Reformed Mission Church in South Africa, was interviewed in his home outside Cape Town.

Jim Wallis: *You have said that you received a great deal of nurture from your family, your home, and your church. How did these lay a foundation for you in your early years?*

Allan Boesak: The family is the basis of all, I think. I was seven years old when my father died. That was too soon, I thought. I still think so. After that my mother took the responsibility in almost every way.

Also the church has always played a very important role. I was very lucky to be the second youngest of eight children in a home where we had daily Bible readings and prayer. And we got to really know the Bible, and we would talk about the biblical stories and the meaning of faith.

We have always believed that the Bible is a basic source of strength and comfort for the whole family. And when you're really poor, then the biblical story is not just another story. When it is applied to your life, often in the very powerful way that it was in our lives, it becomes very, very meaningful; in fact, one of the very few meaningful things in your life.

When I was ten years old, I joined the Association for Christian Students, which also nurtured me. I remember going to "beach missions" during our summer holiday. We had church services for the kids in the morning, and in the evening we had services for everyone in big, big tents.

One morning, the woman who was supposed to do the children's service didn't appear. And Chris Wessels, a school teacher who had quite a formative influence on my life, said, "Let Allan tell them a story and give his testimony."

I don't think anybody took it too seriously when I got up in the pulpit, which we built from sand. But I told people how I came to love the Lord. I cannot remember any specific date or angelic visitation or anything like that. But I just remember growing up and learning to love the Lord in a way that, even at that stage, I knew I would not want to give up—ever.

And they loved it. So day after day, I gave my testimony. I guess part of my love for preaching came from those times.

Wallis: *So this was your first sermon, at the age of ten?*

Boesak: No, it wasn't my first sermon. I preached before that—but to captive audiences. When I was four or five, I would make some of my sisters sit down with their dolls and I would preach. When I would go to church with my family, my mother says I would cry if I couldn't take the biggest hymnbook, the Bible, and two other books because I saw the minister coming into the pulpit with these books. And that's what I wanted to be like.

From my mother I learned that the widow and the fatherless are in the special care of God. She believed that passionately. Otherwise there wouldn't be so many stories about how God made that promise come true in the Bible.

So when today I say, "It is true; God is the God of the poor and the widow and the fatherless—and God does call them to stand where he stands, namely for justice and against injustice," people say, "Oooh, that's liberation theology." And I say,

"That's fine. It may be liberation theology; but that's what I learned at home."

Wallis: *There's a story about your mother and how she put this sense of God protecting the widow and the orphaned and the poor into action at one point.*

Boesak: After my father died, we bought this very old and dilapidated house. We spent weekends trying to patch up this old house. My mother bought bricks from a builder, who was a fairly well-off man. When he delivered the bricks, she counted them. Instead of the four hundred she had paid for, he had given her only about 250.

So she called him up and said, "You did not give me all the bricks. Where are the rest?"

He said, "Don't bother me with this. I know that my men delivered all the bricks."

He was a man, he was rich, he was powerful, so he just told her. And she told him, "I will never forget this. But that's okay, you don't have to worry about the bricks. The God I believe in is the protector of the widow and the fatherless. And somehow you're going to know that." Then she put the phone down, and said, "All right, let's work with the bricks we've got. And maybe then we will have to save a little more and buy some more bricks."

A week or two later, this man came up to the house and delivered the rest of the bricks. "What happened?" my mother asked.

"Well," he said, "something did happen." He was building houses and one or two of them had mysteriously caught on fire. And he interpreted this as a sign from heaven.

He didn't say much. He must have been incredibly embarrassed, and a little bit fearful, I think, of my mother. She is very small, not an impressive person, and not educated at all; she only went to elementary school. She was a seamstress and at that stage worked for three rands and fifty cents [about $2] a week.

But I saw all this, at age twelve, and it made a tremendous impression on me because I saw that in a very tangible way, God does take care of the poor and the meek and the lowly and the oppressed. That was something I was never to forget for the rest of my life.

So today I am literally impassioned about these things. I keep on telling people that this is the biblical message and that it doesn't matter what the situation looks like; God will make true the promises that God has made. And there is no doubt in my mind that God will.

Wallis: *Education was very important for you. You did well. And you began to encounter obstacles as your mind and heart carried you further.*

Boesak: Education was very important. That was just about the only thing my mother always said they could not take away from me.

When I got to seminary, however, I began to get the feeling that what I received there was not good enough. The theology training course was five years—and at the end of it, your highest diploma was still your high school diploma. There was no degree, no specific academic acknowledgment, and you would not be recognized by any academic institution.

We were the so-called—and I hate these terms, but one has to use them—colored folk of the Dutch Reformed Church. And we had been kicked out of the white church. Our professors were not academics or teachers. They were all white and steeped in the theology of the white Dutch Reformed Church where justification of apartheid came as naturally to them as drinking water.

When we pleaded to be allowed to take correspondence courses through the University of South Africa, where we could study for a degree, they refused. Their reasoning was, "You don't need this kind of study. If there is any academic study to be done, it will be done by people of the white church."

One professor said, "You cannot include things like Greek and Hebrew in your curriculum because at Stellenbosch University the students fail like flies. And if the white students have difficulties, what in the world do you think you would do? You are just not capable of doing that kind of study."

I remember that I was never so enraged as at that moment. I remember also vowing to myself that I would not accept this. I would prove him wrong no matter what it took.

In 1965 James McCord, president of Princeton Seminary, and my immediate predecessor as president of the World Alliance [of Reformed Churches], came to South Africa. He was invited by the white church, but they squeezed in one little lecture at our seminary. I asked him a few questions.

After the lecture he called me up, and he said, "Young man, I like the way you phrased those questions." We talked a little bit and he said, "How would you like a scholarship to Princeton?" I almost flipped. I said, "Sure!"

One professor went with me to the board of professors to discuss the scholarship, and they told him, "Forget it." What made the board particularly angry was that, at that time, Princeton had a requirement that if a student from a Third World church came to study at Princeton, his church had to send a letter stating that this training would help equip this person for a position of leadership in the church.

The board members were so scared of that sentence. They didn't intend to have any black leadership at all. So that sentence, even more than the specter of my coming back with some academic degree, frightened them.

In the same way, a scholarship to Hamburg University had to be turned down. In 1968 I was ordained, and in 1969 I began to look for places to study. In 1970, at the invitation of Beyers Naudé at the Christian Institute, Professor Johannes Verkuyl from Holland came to South Africa and preached in my church. He said, "My goodness, you really should come and study in Holland."

Despite great difficulties, I decided to go. When I wrote my seminary and asked them for a letter of recommendation, they refused me even that. I went out of this country with my wife and my six-week-old baby. We had to sell everything we had in the house and borrow money.

But we went without a cent from this church, without a word of encouragement, without a letter of recommendation. In fact, in the last telephone conversation I had with one professor, he told me, "You can go to Holland. But I'm telling you, your future in this church is over. You are finished."

But I had my vow. I came back.

I returned in 1976, and we had our next synod in 1978. I

challenged one white minister who pontificated about the impossibility of church unity.

He quoted a text in Isaiah that says, "They who believe shall not hasten." His interpretation of the text was that if we believe in church unity, that's fine, but we must not be in too much of a hurry.

I got up and said, "Do you know that the same word that has been translated in that Isaiah passage as 'shall not hasten' can also be translated 'shall not run away'? And we shall also not run away from this challenge." I told him, "If you go back and check your Hebrew, you will see that I am right."

And the elders spontaneously applauded and came to me and said, "Oh, it's so wonderful to see one of our own people." Here was someone out of their own midst, from a little place in the Northwestern Cape—which would be like rural Alabama in the United States—and that is why they were so proud.

And that is why the white *Dutch Reformed Church Journal*, after my election in 1982, wrote, "The most bitter pill to swallow is that this man, this little brown man, with his degree from Holland and his Dutch accent, is now the president of the World Alliance for the Reformed Church." And when I saw that, I thought, "Oh, this is all right. We actually have them where we want them. They can't stand it."

So I made true my vow. And what was even more important was that I opened the door for others to get training.

Wallis: *How has the church evolved into its current role?*

Boesak: My church had never said anything meaningful about apartheid, never condemned it. In 1978 we did for the first time. Once that was said, everything was placed in focus: the role of the white church; the role of the white so-called missionaries in our church; the role of the acquiescent, older black ministers; the role of the younger generation.

It was such a pleasure to preach to congregations, to write, and to simply show how the Bible was being distorted and abused by the white church and by the white missionaries in our church to suit the apartheid ideology. It was a marvelous thing to see how the eyes of the church opened up. In the Synod of 1978 we just said, "Apartheid is a sin."

By 1982 we talked about the secular gospel of apartheid. And, on the basis of that, we accused the white Dutch Reformed Church of heresy and announced the "status confessionis," or state of confession, and called for repentance.

"Status confessionis" is a term that was used by the World Alliance and has been adopted by our church. Certainly for Christians in the Reformed tradition, we believe that there comes a time in history when a situation becomes more than a political argument.

Because of the bankrupt political situation apartheid brings, and the immense suffering it brings, it is a political situation. But there is more at stake. Apartheid, after all, was first conceived of in the church. And the church was used as the model for the state. Apartheid is seen and defended as a Christian policy that expresses the will of God for this country.

The people who created and maintain this policy all call themselves Christians. Moreover, they stand in the same Reformed tradition that we do. What we are uncovering here is more than a political fallacy; it is a distortion of the gospel of Jesus Christ, something that has poisoned the body of Christ in its essence in this country.

For us, of course, it's extremely painful because apartheid began in the Dutch Reformed Church in the nineteenth century and was implemented first around the table of the Lord when white Christians said, "We can take anything, but we will no longer drink with these slaves and former slaves out of one cup and share the one bread in the one church."

So this moment, when we express the unity of the body of Christ in the death of Jesus and the love that God has for us, has become the issue on which racism is based in the Dutch Reformed Church.

Our struggle is one for the integrity of the gospel and of the very life of the church itself. It is a moment of faith, a moment of confession. We are placed in a state of confession over against this false gospel, this blasphemous plague.

When a church speaks like this—and we were the first in this country to do so—it goes beyond any other statement. In a sense, once you have said this, then all other statements about apartheid become superfluous. You must now act on the basis of this confession. And it is out of that background that we became the first church in the Dutch Reformed tradition of Holland and this country, in almost four hundred years, to add a new confession to the three traditional ones. And that was the Confession of Belhar.

I think, for the Dutch Reformed Church, it was a moment of rebirth. If we fail the Lord now, on this point, and if we now bow down to the forces of threat and intimidation, and if we accept now the evil of apartheid, we would be far more guilty in the eyes of God than the white Dutch Reformed Church could ever be. All of the major churches in this country accepted the heresy declaration. This pushed the churches further into the struggle.

So this constant claim that what is being done here is being done in the name of Jesus Christ, I think, could and should be seen as the basis for the state-church conflict in South Africa, because we have to say two things. We have to say that this system cannot be called Christian. That's blasphemy. We have to resist it. And we have to say, "Jesus Christ is Lord," over against the government that even in those days began to make absolute, totalitarian claims and expected the churches to accept it very quietly.

Then things escalated, because after 1983 the United Democratic Front [UDF] began. The churches were confronted with the challenge that the people in the pews would go out and join the UDF and fully participate in marches. We had said as churches in 1979 that we must engage in acts of civil disobedience as an act of obedience to God. But the only people who were willing to do that were the people in the United Democratic Front.

So there was a serious gap between what the church said and believed and what we were actually able or willing to do. We were scared in the churches. Church leaders were not ready then.

Then came the attack on the South African Council of Churches, and we had to be very clear where we stood and how we were going to take up this challenge from the South African government. Then in 1985 came the state of emergency, and the churches became the only safe places where people could meet.

At that stage, again, the church leaders did not take a very active, overtly political role. The churches did make their buildings available for meetings, until it became clear that the government didn't care if meetings were in churches or not.

You have heard about people being arrested in church while we were in a prayer meeting for detainees. And how they came one time and arrested the whole congregation—fathers, mothers, children, babies—everybody. How they shot tear gas into churches, including my own. And how our candlelight services were declared a threat to the security of the state; even the burning of a candle was seen to be subversive. But when we asked the church leaders to join us in 1985 in a nonviolent march, none of them came.

Now, all of the political organizations have been banned. And before we were really ready, the churches were catapulted to the front line. There we were, in the trenches, unprepared as we were. Unprepared because, in spite of all those statements, we were never really serious about getting into the business of resisting the government. In spite of saying apartheid is a heresy, many of the church leaders and many of the churches are still not ready to say the government is illegitimate.

St. Augustine was right when he said, "A government without justice is little more than a gang of bandits." I think this is what we are facing in this country. And now, all of a sudden, things are happening. I have never seen such unanimity among the church leaders. I have never seen such resolve. They came together the day we heard the organizations were banned.

What happened as a result of the banning of the organizations? On Wednesday, February 24, 1988, when we heard the news, we said we had to have a meeting because this is very serious. Archbishop Tutu and I had a press conference that same day and decided to call Frank Chikane and ask whether he would call a meeting of church leaders. He did.

The church leaders then decided, "Yes, we will come to Cape Town. On Monday we will have a church service in the cathedral and we will march." They came together for the first time, more than twenty-five church leaders, five hundred clergy. It was beautiful.

And I had said, "You know, I realize that there are some of you who will not have everybody with you in your church. All of us may be in that position; but some of you have many white members who may be far more angry at you than my black members who disagree with me would ever be. So we will understand if you will not participate." But they came.

And after they were hosed down and had been arrested, we got together for the press conference, and they said, "We will do this again. We have to do this again." I haven't seen anything like that.

Things escalated after that. The newspapers attacked us. The government attacked us. The Dutch Reformed Church attacked us, singling out Bishop Tutu, Frank Chikane, and myself. The church leaders responded, saying, "You're not only talking about them." The Anglican church responded. My church committee responded. Canterbury sent an envoy. The World Council of Churches sent messages. We still get messages from churches all over the world every day. My own presbytery responded, pledging support and further action.

And the thing has just escalated further. P. W. Botha has now threatened to take action against us. They have tried to isolate us from the rest of the churches. But that will also prove to be futile.

So we are into a very different phase now. Since 1985 the government has been trying to draw the bottom line. And every time there's a new bottom line.

The state of emergency was a bottom line for them. Thousands of people have been in jail at one time. Hundreds of our people are being killed.

After two years the government must have thought, "By now we've surely broken the back of the democratic opposition." And much to their surprise, they found out that the opposition was still there. Very much still there. Then they decided to ban the organizations. And then the churches stepped in. And now they have to act against the churches, so it's a new bottom line.

This shows the utter desperation of the government and the strength and the resilience of the movement. I think now is a very decisive phase.

What is happening here reminds me of 1933 to 1934 in Germany. Hitler never wanted a Nazi church. All he wanted was an apolitical, acquiescent church that would not challenge the government. A church that would not raise its voice when the trade unions were hit, when the communists were singled out, when the Jews were persecuted. And that's the kind of church Hitler got.

And so I am not surprised when I hear [moderator of the Dutch Reformed Church] Johan Heyns say, "I'm not defending the government, all I'm saying is that Boesak and Tutu must accept the authority of the government." All they want from us is to be silent.

That is what this modern Hitler in South Africa is getting from the white Dutch Reformed Church. The choices the church is facing in this country are exactly the same choices that the churches in Germany faced. And that is why it is important that not only individuals stand up and be counted, but that the church as the church stand up and speak.

In Germany, Hitler won because the institutions of the people succumbed. The church as an institution succumbed. The Niemoellers, the Bonhoeffers, and the Karl Barths, Hitler could handle. Say they're not part of the church. Isolate Bonhoeffer and hang him. Isolate Niemoeller and throw him in jail. Isolate Karl Barth and send him back to Switzerland. That he could do because the church as the body of Christ did not move. And here we must not let that happen.

Wallis: *The South African government is saying, "Boesak, Tutu, and Chikane are the problems. They are political. They are communists, or at least supportive of communist, atheist, violent revolution. They are not the real church." How are the churches at the grassroots responding to that charge?*

Boesak: I'm actually not worried at all. I think the churches are very clear where we are and where we should be. I don't think the people would allow them to isolate us. But they don't understand that, because the white church of which P. W. Botha is a member doesn't know anymore what it is to be the church.

The white Dutch Reformed Church rests upon their power — the power over the media, the access their leaders have to the press. Our statements explaining that their attacks on us are wrong don't even get published. Behind them is the full and absolute power of the South African government, the strongest economic and military power on the continent, with powerful connections in Washington, London, Bonn, and Paris. So when Heyns stands up to speak in the white Dutch Reformed Church, that is his basis.

When I stand up, there is no access to the media here to explain to my people. There is no power of propaganda, no guns, no powerful armies or governments or laws behind me. All I have, literally, is the word of God that tells me about the promises of this God, the story that I have carried in my heart from childhood on. And I have the faith of the people in front of me because that is all they have, too.

The white Dutch Reformed Church has faith in power. They don't have faith in the suffering Jesus Christ who came into this world. His clothes were gambled away. His identification with the poor and the meek and the lowly came to that point on the cross. How can they identify with him? How can they understand him? How can they hear him?

And that is why it is impossible for the white Dutch Reformed Church to say with us that simple text from the Bible: "You have to be more obedient to God than to human beings." Because if they say that, they have to sever their relationship with this government. And they can't.

Even while we know the situation is so grim that you can step outside and be arrested, and that your pastor can be thrown in jail or worse in the coming week, we can still come together with a joy that is almost indescribable. That experience P. W. Botha and the others don't know anything about. And so that is why it doesn't mean a thing when they say we do not represent the church. Because they do not understand what it means to be the church.

Wallis: *Tell us about your own experience. There have been very specific, threatening attacks directed at your home, your office, your family, your own life.*

Boesak: Yes. We've had these threats before. But the situation in the country was different then.

Years ago I had an experience. This white man came to my door, and he said, "I have been in prayer and fasting for a week or two now. God told me about what a danger you are to this country. He also told me that you would have to die and I would be your executioner if you don't stop this."

That was the first time I had been faced physically with something like that. I remember just standing there trembling. I didn't even say anything back to him. I just closed the door and leaned against it. And my son Allan, then two years old, came running up the passage. As I hugged him, I understood for the first time, I think, what I was doing to my family.

I was completely shaken up. And I found that I had to pray out loud. I couldn't just say the words in my heart, because I was afraid that if I didn't hear the words, I wouldn't be able to keep them. I had to hear myself say it, so that I could be held accountable.

Now death squads are something that we've become used to. Friends have been murdered quite cold-bloodedly. I said to the church, "You ought to know there have been threats. You ought to know also that I'm not a particularly brave person. But I do feel that what we're doing is the call of the gospel."

I'm not being callous in terms of my family. But I cannot change now. I cannot give up now. I understand my political engagement to be at the very heart of my discipleship.

I said to my church, "I have no other weapon but the will of God. And that will remain so. If I die, it will not be because I wanted a bloody revolution. Revolution, yes. Radical change in this country, yes. But it will not be because I wanted to kill people. It will not be because I called upon anybody to hate P. W. Botha or the police or any white person, for that matter. It will be because I have tried to stand up for justice. I have tried to be true and faithful to Jesus Christ in this situation."

In our country you must not say, "Why me?" Rather, the time has come for us to say, "Why not me?" And I'm not morbid about this. I have come to peace with it. I have faced guns and the police numerous times. I have preached in a church literally with a policeman standing next to me holding a gun to my head.

Oh, I would love to live a little longer. I enjoy life immensely. I enjoy my music. I enjoy my friends. I enjoy my family. I live with a zest that I don't want to give up. But I also know, again to quote Martin King, it is very, very true: "There are some things so dear and so precious and so eternally true that they are worth dying for. And if you are not willing to die for those things, then you are really not fit to live." Only people who know that they might have to die for something that is indeed eternally true and precious, I think, know how to live.

What is a greater joy than to work for justice, to seek peace, to stand up for things that are worthwhile? To plead for the fatherless, the widow, and the poor, to take up their cause and fight for it, and to work for the realization of the kingdom of God. What is greater joy than that?

Wallis: *Even with these threats, I would say that there is more life and joy and love and just taking simple pleasure—with life and each other—in this house than most houses I've been in.*

Boesak: Yes. Whatever happens, these are the moments the children are going to remember the most. The atmosphere is what they're going to remember. I've often said that if you're afraid, then you die a thousand times before you die. And I wouldn't want my children to die little deaths every day of their lives.

You cannot really prepare anybody for what might happen, certainly not your children. I still find it extremely difficult to talk to them about what they need to know. But they need to understand what their father is about. They cannot only see the crowds who love me. They must also see those who hate me, and they must understand why.

Wallis: *I think they do understand. And yet Allan, Jr., is doing handstands all over the house, and there are soccer games and tennis matches and dance classes. All of this is going on in the midst of this intense political situation with all the threats.*

Boesak: This is sustenance, you know. It must be like that. If I didn't have this, and the church, I guarantee I wouldn't be able to do what I'm doing right now. So in a sense P. W. might have more understanding than people would give him credit for. If he could actually separate me from the church and from my family, then they know they wouldn't even have to kill me. I would just wither away and die. They know that. The wonderful thing is, they can't do that. It's impossible.

Wallis: *As the churches have taken on this unprecedented role, the government has been very publicly responsive. How do you perceive the government's response? And what is the role of the Dutch Reformed Church?*

Boesak: I believe that the government was taken totally by surprise by the churches' action. They did not ever think the churches would come together and take on the government as we did. And frankly speaking, I must admit I was a little surprised too.

The government realized immediately that if you tackle the churches, this is a totally new ball game. This is not simply protest against the government or resistance to evil, although it is that. It is a question for us, finally, and ultimately, of obedience to God. I don't think the government thought that it would come to this.

Then the Dutch Reformed Church reacts with the government and says, "Tutu and Boesak claim that they are the church, but they are not the church." Then they go one step further. They claim to be the true church. It is preposterous.

This is an old trick, of course. Whenever the state wants to move against an institution, an organization, or people who have links with the church, then the state accuses us of not really being Christian. That accusation is almost always followed by some statement by the white Dutch Reformed Church saying, "Yes, indeed, those people are not Christians, they are not the church. They do not represent anybody. They are merely politicians using the gospel." This opens the way for the state to act against such people.

As most of those cabinet ministers and government people enter white Dutch Reformed Churches across the country on Sunday morning, they are being told, "Whatever you have done between Monday and Saturday, you have done because God wants it." It is the perfect role of the false prophets of the court in the Old Testament.

But there may come a time, and maybe the time is now, that someone will have to ask the question, "Can you be church in this country and also be what the Dutch Reformed Church is?" I think this is probably the next step, not simply in terms of the confrontation between the state and the church, but the confrontation between the church and the church in this country.

Wallis: *How do you see this church-state and church-church conflict to be evolving?*

Boesak: All I can see is that we are only at the beginning of the conflict. There will be much more confrontation between the state and the church, and between us and the white Dutch Reformed Church.

Out of this will crystallize the true nature of the South African government. It will quite openly become less and less the servant of God from Romans 13, and more and more the beast from Revelation 13.

As the church challenges this beast and as the confrontation grows, and as the testimony to the Lordship of Jesus Christ becomes more and more and more costly, many in the church will deny the Lord rather than stand up in the face of persecution. Many will find solace in acquiescence. Many will run into a kind of neutral ground, not understanding there is no neutral ground anymore.

We have arrived at the time of the apocalypse. Either you are willing to testify with the prophet on an abandoned, isolated island, or you give in to the powers of destruction and are lured away by those who can buy you off.

The church in South Africa is facing a new phase of persecution. What we have seen over the last few years will intensify— pastors being thrown in jail, hundreds of Christians going to jail, church services being broken up with guns and dogs and tear gas, and whole congregations being arrested. As the end draws near for this government, and as white people genuinely begin to realize that the days of white domination are just about over, I think their sense of desperation and panic will grow. And there will be for us, as the persecution increases, the temptation to become more and more like the oppressor.

The government is trying to force upon us the only options that are at this moment open to them. They are trying to close down all options for us and make us believe that we are just like them in that respect—that we only have two options: either to accept apartheid for what it is and resign ourselves to it, or to opt for violence, because that's what they have done.

They resign themselves to apartheid, and say, "We will defend this position with all of the violence we can muster." They don't have any other choice. Apartheid would not exist for one minute without the awesome violence that is needed to maintain the system. And I think they are trying to get the churches to believe that that is what is left for us as well.

I have been pleading to our people, and to the church in particular, let us not succumb to this temptation to believe that these are the only options open to us. It seems to me now, more than ever before, it is incumbent upon us to carve out new possibilities, because without these possibilities this country will not survive.

This government is bent not only on the destruction of this country, but it is bent on the destruction of our whole future. It cannot even understand dreams of justice and equality and human dignity and humanity. Those things are already beyond their grasp.

The only people who have that dream in their hearts and can keep it alive are the oppressed. It is the duty of the church to see to it that that dream is kept alive. Those ideals that people have been dying for in this country for so long will be the foundation upon which the new South Africa will be built.

Because all avenues of nonviolent protest have been shut down, because the government is so incredibly violent and brutal, I fear also for the brutalization of the soul of our people. We will become just like them if we're not careful.

I have understanding for people who, in their desperation, look for violent solutions to the problem. And I will not judge them; I have been in this situation for too long. We all have been knee-deep in blood. And I have seen the incredible cruelty of the people who run this country.

There is a very basic human response to this: revenge. People will say, "The only language they understand is the language of violence." But if you choose violence from a strategic point of view, you make it so easy for them, because violence is just about the only thing they know how to do well.

But also our very soul is at stake. We will be destroyed. We would come out victorious in the end, some people argue, because we are so many—no white government can kill thirty million black people.

But even if we survive, even if we reach the other side of this battle through that necessary river of blood, what will be at the other end of it?

All through history I see that people who build their future on violence find it hard to understand that there are any other true solutions. At the simplest provocation, they fall back onto the solution of violence.

And only years later do we begin to understand that violence really does not give any solutions at all. It may change a situation, but it does not really transform it. It may destroy the present structure, but it so often also destroys the foundations that are necessary to build a new society.

More and more I've come to understand that Gandhi and Martin and Jesus were right. You don't have to be judgmental about the desperation of oppressed people reaching for a gun, but I will continue to warn my people. We are in danger of losing our souls. We are jeopardizing our future. We are selling out our humanity for a quick victory. We are changing the pain of today for a much deeper malady of tomorrow.

We must try to find ways and means of breaking the cycle of violence. But people who want to talk like that must be willing to wade into that river of blood and fight alongside others without weapons that will kill. They must be willing to take upon themselves the burden of the oppressed in a very real way and to die for the sake of others.

If you're not willing to do that, if you're not willing to take the suffering upon yourself, you must not shun those who are in the midst of the violence. You have to actually go into the battlefield itself and there give your testimony.

I am always a little irritated when people say, "Yes, but you must be willing to dirty your hands in the struggle." It doesn't mean that you dirty your hands only with another's blood that you have spilled. You can also dirty your hands while you take care of the wounded and while you bleed yourself because you are unwilling to hurt or kill another person.

If ever there was a situation to speak of a just revolution, South Africa at this point is it. And it's only when you can make that acknowledgment that you really begin to understand the need for the church to plead for and work for and initiate true, authentic nonviolent resistance.

The more I see the violence, the more I understand the need for breaking the cycle of violence in South Africa. I am more committed to the struggle now than ever before. I'm also more committed to nonviolent action and a nonviolent lifestyle, to try to preserve what is best and noble for our country.

I don't think my leadership is dependent upon the degree to which I'm willing to embrace violence. That's not the way we work. White people, Western people, whose whole history is one of violence and threat and intimidation, may think that way. In the United States, people's whole security, their happiness, depends on having those stockpiles of nuclear weapons to secure, as they say, their "way of life."

I think it is ridiculous apart from being blasphemous. I think it's a sick, cruel joke. If my happiness and my security were to depend on weapons of destruction and the ability of my president to press a button that would destroy God's creation fifty-three times over, I wouldn't sleep one wink.

Many people think you are a leader if you are willing to either lead in violence or accommodate people's natural fears and tendency toward revenge. I'm turning this around. I'm saying to people, "The more you put your faith in violence, the more hopeless and helpless you become."

Just look at white people in this country. They have the best-equipped army on the continent. They also have something else that is necessary to make a good soldier: They are cold-blooded, and they will kill you without thinking twice. And they are rich. But they don't know what it means to have peace of mind. They don't know such a thing as security.

I pity them, because while I don't have their weapons, money, or power, I have peace of mind in the sense that I know that the promises of God are so secure that they can never fail. And I'm willing to take a lot for the sake of this, because I happen to think that if our people would make these values the basis on which we stand, then we will last.

Wallis: *What is the future of South Africa?*

Boesak: In the short run, it's going to be very grim; there's no doubt about that. I think we have to be very sober when we talk about this. There is an evolving white panic that is extremely dangerous and will destroy this country as it is.

It is also extremely dangerous to the region. No one in close range of these people is safe, neither our people in the townships, nor the people in Mozambique, nor Zimbabwe, Angola, or Namibia.

White people are desperate. They've lost everything. They know that in spite of the assurances of the white Dutch Reformed Church, there is no morality left; there is no justification left. They know that they've lost it, and so all they have is the whiteness of their skin and their willingness to use the violence they have at their disposal.

People who are losing their power and their privileges can do strange things. Over the next year or so, you'll see more of what is already taking place: the disintegration of white politics, the disintegration of Afrikanerdom as we have known it over the last decade, and a totally mindless violent bent that will come over this country.

I think that the historian was right when he said, "If you look all over history you'll see that the totalitarian and dictatorial and violent regimes don't decline; they tend to collapse." And I think we're heading for such collapse here. There are too many factors at work in South Africa at the moment.

But I am astounded by the resilience of the oppressed people in this country. Under normal circumstances, the government would have expected that by now there would be no opposition left. And I think under normal circumstances they would have been right. But South Africa's oppressed people—and most of us are Christians— find resources at a depth that the people who rule this country don't even know about.

After two years of a state of emergency, everybody knows that if you go to a church service, for example a service to pray for detainees, you literally take your life in your hands. All the police need to do is to turn a church service into a riot. Then they shut out the world, and they can do what they will. No newspaper will be able to say what happened and who did what to whom. That's the law. But still the people come.

The police and government actually get nervous when you go to jail en masse. One of the rules is that you may not sing. It's a great joy for our people to go into jail and start singing. Oppressed people who can sing must be subversive to any oppressive power. And for our people to experience this in worship as well as on the streets, in the struggle, in political rallies, is a sign of hope that is one of the strongest things that we've got.

One of the reasons why people keep on singing is because of

tradition, but another is because we are more certain of our victory than they can ever be of their endurance. There is no doubt about it.

Some people think you can only believe the victory will come if you know that you're going to be part of it, that you'll actually see it. But your faith in the victory of goodness doesn't have to be tied to your actual participation in that victory. It doesn't matter to me whether I will see it or not. That does not change the truth one iota—that the victory will be there and we will have it.

"I would say that our movement is a movement deeper into God. That is where we touch one another more nearly, as we all grow in our prayerfulness and in our relationship with our Lord."

5

Deeper into God:
Spirituality for the Struggle

An Interview with Desmond Tutu

Desmond Tutu, the Anglican archbishop of Cape Town and winner of the 1984 Nobel Peace Prize, was interviewed at his home in Bishopscourt outside Cape Town.

Jim Wallis: *We would very much like to hear your perspective on what people speak of as the new era for the church in South Africa, the new level in the struggle against apartheid as the church moves to the front lines.*

Desmond Tutu: In many ways the church—perhaps less spectacularly in the past—has been involved in this struggle for some time. Church people have been responsible for bringing the Namibian issue [South Africa's illegal occupation of neighboring Namibia] before the United Nations. And they have brought the plight of squatters very much to the fore.

For instance, the church was involved over the issue of forced population removals, particularly in Magopa, one of the villages that the government "moved." The South African Council of Churches, with a number of church leaders, was there. We went and stood with the people to try to support them at a time when they were under threat.

Perhaps the government had not yet learned how to be thoroughly repressive so that the church did not need, in many ways, to be quite so spectacular. There were other avenues available for people, avenues that were more explicitly political.

What is different, perhaps, now is that the government has progressively eliminated most of the other organizations which legitimately could have been around to articulate the people's concern. And the government's repression has intensified. They have chosen the military option.

I don't think those who are calling the shots in the government are really interested in negotiating any longer. They believe that they've got the military strength and the political strength to deal with any obstructive elements. And they have more or less neutralized most of the opposition.

What is a remarkable feature of this time is the unity that is emerging in the churches. All of us were quite surprised at the broad spectrum that was represented at the February 29, 1988, March on Parliament. It never happened before at that level. It was remarkable.

The decision to march was made just a few days before. We asked people—very, very busy people—to come down to Cape Town. And they dropped everything and came, even with the prospect of being arrested. I don't think the government is aware of what they have unleashed.

Wallis: *How do you explain that?*

Tutu: I would say that what we saw on February 29th is not something that suddenly happened on its own account. It happened because the consciousness of people has been awakened and deepened, as well as because black leadership has been coming to the fore in quite a number of churches. We are seeing here in South Africa the fruit of the work of very many people.

I also have to say that there is something powerful in the fact that people are praying for you. You see, we are representatives of a great army around the world. And when we tell these guys [government leaders] that they've really lost, it's because they really have lost. Those who are for us are many, many times more numerous than those who are for them, and they really ought to join the winning side.

On the march, we were one at a very deep level. We were agreed that this thing [apartheid] is evil. We were agreed about what we were going to do, whatever the consequences.

I was scared. I was sitting in the cathedral before the march, and we were praying. You could have heard the butterflies in my tummy.

Of course, we didn't know how the police were going to react. In fact, at the time that they stopped us and we knelt, this man beckoned to the phalanx of police behind him, and I said, "Well, we'll really get it now. I mean, we're getting the whips and the dogs and we're just going to have to brave it out." One was sort of utterly scared.

We need to remember that, in fact, we belong in a body. It's as if all of us have caught onto a wavelength where we've said [to the government], "That's far enough. No further," but not with any sense of bravado. We are just aware, and maybe more people are aware of the pain of the people.

We who are black have an advantage over those who are white. But I think that a number of whites have come to the experience of seeing some of the pain, and it's carried into their hearts. The fact that the government did what they did [on February 24] in banning those organizations, along with the banning of people who are working for peace, has probably turned the scales.

Wallis: *The confrontation between the church and the South African state has now become a very visible, public confrontation. And you have been again thrust into a very public role, often taking the brunt of attack from the government. You had a meeting with President P. W. Botha. What was that meeting like? And also what is your view about the role in which you find yourself?*

Tutu: I don't think you should over-dramatize my part in it. In many ways it's very incidental. Although individual persons are important, this fight's got nothing, in many ways, to do with individuals. That is the beauty of it, you see. As individuals, we may help to focus things. But, if I were to pass off center stage, it's not going to be the end of this movement. This movement is much, much bigger than Desmond Tutu.

I had a two-part meeting with the state president, P. W. Botha. The first part of the meeting was fairly rational. We talked like we were very civilized human beings, and he was telling me how he operates his exercise of the prerogative [to

Deeper into God

intervene in judicial cases involving charges against police or
army personnel].

At the time it sounded relatively plausible: He does not interfere with the judicial process, except in extremely limited
circumstances. As it turns out, of course, it's nothing of the sort.
He was lying like it was nobody's business.

Then we sort of changed gears from a fairly amicable meeting,
and the temperature dropped several degrees because he then
came to his point that it was I who was persuading people to
break the law and so forth. He's fond of becoming, as it were,
a heavy-handed, scolding headmaster.

I was going to be very subdued, very calm.

I could have kept quiet, but I decided I might never get this
chance again. Our people had suffered so long. I said, "One
thing you've got to know is that I'm not a small boy. You're not
my headmaster."

But we did get into like little boys, really. It was a shame,
accusations and counteraccusations, that sort of thing. I thought,
he's certainly never heard this from a black this way.

I don't know whether that's how Jesus would have handled
it. But at that moment I didn't quite mind how Jesus would have
handled it. I was going to handle it my way. I hope that is how
he would have handled it, because it was done on behalf of
people who have been hurt by these guys.

I told him, "I love this country, probably more personally than
you, because our people fought against the Nazis. You didn't."
He got very, very angry about that. But it is true—I mean they
[the National Party] supported the Nazis.

As for the church's role, the weakness in what we have been
about as a church is that we've been so episodic. We do one
little thing here, and one there, but there is no sustained effort.

One of the things we need to do is take up seriously this
whole question of nonviolence. We are amateurs at nonviolent
action. All we've been doing really is preaching it, and it's not
been a truly viable alternative to violence. We've spoken as if
just to exhort people is enough; whereas if they were to see that
we're serious about this, then people would begin to think that
it is a credible program that we are suggesting.

One of the things that we need to be looking at is the possibility of nonviolent action in places where the government is forcibly relocating people. If we can manage to be with the people, say, for a week, that would be a positive step. We may not, in fact, stop the government from doing anything, but we may get in the way or in the works a little bit, and publicity would accrue to a situation. If we went there for one day and stood between the people and the bulldozers, that would be the kind of thing that we ought to be thinking about.

Wallis: *So you're hoping the Parliament March won't be just an isolated event or episode in the church's witness but part of a sustained and growing effort.*

Tutu: We hope so. We think public acts of witness give encouragement to the people and make the authorities aware that we are serious. The authorities are going to have to reckon with the fact that they will probably have to put us into jail.

Wallis: *You have said that you think the churches are more ready than ever before to act in this kind of way. What do you think will happen if not just a few church leaders but the masses of church people really begin to act?*

Tutu: We need to take into account that there is probably some distance between the leadership and the bulk of the church membership. But certainly the black church is waiting to be mobilized.

My concern—and I think it would be the concern of many church leaders—is that I would not be able to deal with my conscience, if, for instance, we go out on the streets, and in a mass action the soldiers shoot their guns. They are more likely to shoot if it is a black crowd than if it is a few prominent church leaders.

One important thing is if we can mobilize the white congregations. I think that there are some who are straining at the leash, who see that what we've got is unsatisfactory, and who see that the prospects for the future are not good. Down the road, unless we have radical change, there's not really a future for them and their children. And now they are ready to participate in trying to bring about change.

I think we have a vicious and ruthless government, and they would mow people down like flies. If they give a gun to a white policeman and the target is black, you don't have to spend a split second wondering what he'll do. But it's less likely if there are white people as well.

Wallis: *What do you see in the immediate future for the church leaders in South Africa's struggle?*

Tutu: We have the problem of what to do with the people who say we are wasting time, that we've got to use violence. I think the only way that our credibility can be maintained is if they see that we are not leading from behind, that we are involved and are prepared to take risks, and that we are in the struggle for the long haul. And we ought to prepare ourselves for that.

We've got to get down to the business of training as many people as possible in nonviolent action and its spirituality. We must be seen as being quite prepared to take the consequences of standing up on behalf of God's people.

Wallis: *This is more than a political struggle, it's also a spiritual struggle. What kind of spiritual resources and strength must be drawn upon to continue the struggle?*

Tutu: First, I think one has to say God is pretty smart, because we have an interrelatedness in the body of Christ. So we are not alone. There is a bigger movement, and we are buoyed up and carried by the fervor and the love and the prayers of so many people.

There are extraordinary prayers that are offered by the church—the nuns, the contemplatives who spend all of their lives praying, the old ladies, the old gentlemen, people who are sick in hospitals who have learned to be able to offer their pain as part of our Lord's sacrifice, making up, as Paul says, what is lacking in the sufferings of Christ. That is a very, very crucial part of our struggle.

It isn't my struggle, it isn't even the struggle of the people of South Africa. It's the struggle of all the people of God.

And that is what makes us so bold to know that we can't fail. It doesn't depend on me. It's not something that relies on how wonderful you are. Paul puts it very, very well: The foolishness of God is wiser than the wisdom of men.

For those of us who are from a sacramental church our strength is in the encounter with God in the Eucharist, the encounter with God in meditation, the encounter with God in those quiet moments when you're consciously aware of being in the flow. You're being carried along in the current.

But sometimes there are moments when you are in the depths, or you just have to say to God, "God, I am tired." At those times I throw myself into the stream of faith, and I'm carried along in the prayers, and not just of those on earth.

That is the wonder of the community of saints: I think the prayers of all of those who have gone before are working for us as well. Our cries and our joys and our bewilderments—all of those are taken up in this tremendous offering of our Lord and Savior Jesus Christ. That is our spirituality.

Wallis: *Even when you talk about these grim and painful realities, you speak as a person of great hope.*

Tutu: Wouldn't you be? Nothing can be more hopeless than Good Friday; but then Sunday happens. You can't but be a prisoner of hope. And you also meet so many wonderful people, people who have suffered and remained faithful.

One such person is a man I met when I was praying with the people in Mogopa one night. Now this is someone whose house was going to be demolished the next day. Clinics, churches, and shops had been demolished already. And people were going to be moved at the point of a gun. And he got up, and he prayed, in the middle of the night, "God, thank you for loving us."

You couldn't have heard a more nonsensical prayer in the middle of that kind of situation. And yet, here was a man who didn't seem to know any theology but who could offer a prayer of thanksgiving.

Wallis: *As you know, you have tremendous support and love and care from U.S. churches. And Christians in our country will want to know how they can be in solidarity as you move deeper into the struggle.*

Tutu: We relish and revel in the fact of their love and their prayers, and please let them know we are deeply grateful.

I would say that our movement is a movement deeper into God. That is where we touch one another more nearly, as we all grow in our prayerfulness and in our relationship with our Lord. The closer we are to God, obviously, the closer we are to one another. That is the greatest thing that can happen between our churches.

I would say, let them go into the depths with us. Let's walk that way together, deepening our relationship with our Lord. And God will be making them more and more sensitive as to what must happen.

"It is our faith that gives us hope. We know that in our helplessness we become more dependent on God. In our powerlessness we become powerful. It is our weakness that is our strength."

6

Through the Cross:
The South African Church's
Painful Path to Victory

An Interview with Frank Chikane

Frank Chikane, general secretary of the South African Council of Churches, was interviewed in his home in Soweto.

Jim Wallis: *You're now the general secretary of the South African Council of Churches — it was a long road that brought you to this place. Tell us about your background.*

Frank Chikane: I grew up in the Apostolic Faith Mission, a conservative, almost fundamentalist, Pentecostal church which later trained me as a pastor. After my ordination, the church began to accuse me of being involved in politics. I had been asked to address a student conference on Christianity and the political situation, and the press picked it up.

The church council produced its file of press cuttings as evidence against me. I still have the letter which says, "You are suspended from pastoral work because you are involved in politics, because you appeared in the press." I was suspended for one year, from 1981 to 1982; I spent eight months of that time in detention.

After my suspension, I joined the Catholic Institute for Contextual Theology, where I spent five and a half years. That experience was very significant. I had started with a very conservative, highly pietistic theology that could justify and accept the status quo; a pastor's job was to prepare people to go to heaven. But then I was confronted by the reality of the oppressive system, which made me raise new questions that were not answered by my training or tradition.

It was extraordinary for me, from the Apostolic Faith Mission, to be appointed general secretary of the Catholic Institute for Contextual Theology. Given the church I'm from, it's even more extraordinary that I was appointed to be general secretary of the South African Council of Churches, because my church decided in 1975 not to join the Council of Churches. To quote a letter the church circulated after my appointment, the Council of Churches "produces violence and liberation theology to Marxists and Communists."

During my suspension I argued that my church's interpretation of politics is anything that opposes the system. If you do not oppose the system, it's not politics. You can have P. W. Botha addressing you, but you cannot have [Oliver] Tambo [of the African National Congress] because that's politics.

P. W. Botha's letters [see his letters in the appendix] and the statement from the Dutch Reformed Church are saying exactly the same thing: There is the spiritual realm and the political realm. And if you interfere with the political, you are moving away from what is spiritual and Christian.

But I believe you cannot separate religion from the life experience of people. I do not believe that Jesus Christ came for spiritual human beings rather than concrete human beings who live within a particular historical experience. You have to live your life on that farm or in that township, and your Christianity is tested by how you handle that reality.

Some think you can lead a spiritual life outside your experience. That's why people continue to oppress others. Some Christians don't see anything wrong in exploiting farm workers, because they think those actions are outside the spiritual realm; so they can still go to church on Sunday and do their spiritual thing.

Wallis: *So your conservative evangelical background did provide* *you a faith and a biblical foundation that you use against the system now.*

Chikane: I don't regret growing up in the Apostolic Faith Mission because the church has a particular quality of spirituality which helps you to survive. When I sat in the jail cell, I needed to refer back to that spirituality. I needed to say that there is something more than the life I am living here.

I had to be able to say to the guy who tortured me, who happens to be a deacon of my church in the white congregation, "For me to live is Christ, to die is gain. If you kill me, I go to heaven, and it doesn't solve your problem. But if you release me, then I continue preaching the gospel. It does not matter which way you take it, because both ways you're going to be a loser."

They said to me, "You're going to die slowly but surely. Why not decide quickly what you want to do?"

And I said to them, "Well, you also have to make your decision, because I'm not going to change my mind. If you put me under pressure hoping to change my mind, I might die, you see. And you might not have planned to kill me. So you need to make your decision whether in fact you want to kill me or not."

You could easily be suicidal when you are subjected to torture. The torturers actually say, "Why not commit suicide, because you're going to die in a terrible way."

And I said, "No, I'm not going to deprive you of the responsibility of my death."

When you sit in that jail cell, you realize you aren't in control of the world. And that spirituality, that sense of your own limits and dependence on the Lord, which could be seen as a traditional theological position, is very helpful. And that's why I have kept my membership with the church. And I worship there every Sunday.

Wallis: *How often have you been detained and under what circumstances?*

Chikane: I've been detained five times since 1977. The first one was in January 1977, for seven days. Within an hour after my first detention, I couldn't walk. They used brutal, third-degree methods of torture. And then I was detained again from June 1977 until January 1978, and I went through six weeks of torture. It was during that detention that the deacon of my church in the white congregation supervised the fifty-hour period where I was interrogated around-the-clock. During the forty-eighth hour, when I realized the torture was affecting my mental state, I told him, "I'm not going to answer any more questions. You can do what you want to." And they tried for two more hours and then got me out of the chains and dropped me in solitary confinement, where they ignored me for six months.

But that deacon simply believed that he was doing his work. He knows I'm the pastor of a church. But he believes he's stopping the communists and the terrorists of this country. Whites in this country are worried about a Marxist takeover; we are worried about a Christian government which oppresses other Christians.

In 1980 I was detained for a short moment simply because P. W. Botha was coming to the area. The longest detention was from 1981 to 1982. Then during the 1985 UDF [United Democratic Front] treason trial I was detained for two and a half months.

Wallis: *It seems the role of the church has changed a good deal since your ordination.*

Chikane: The missionary church—which for a long time was the main channel of the church in South Africa—consisted of European and American missionaries who were on the side of the colonizers and therefore couldn't see the evils of the system. At worst, they directly supported the system; at best, they took a liberal position of saying, "Don't be excessive if you oppress them."

In the 1960s, when [ANC leader Nelson] Mandela was sentenced to prison and other people were jailed and organizations were banned, the churches supported the government.

But then in the 1970s, the Black Consciousness Movement came into the picture. More and more black people took up leadership roles. By 1975 the shade of the Council of Churches was shifting completely, with more black presence. And now it is a true reflection of the population distribution in the country—it is 80 percent black.

Now the church is beginning to reflect critically on the reality of the situation, and it is able to take a prophetic position. You don't often find a church or church structure—particularly an ecumenical structure—declaring a government illegitimate. But the South African Council of Churches last year declared this government illegitimate and said that we are not obliged to obey these unjust laws.

The conditions in the country—the level of brutality, the pain and suffering that ordinary church people see—move them to think in a more critical way about the system and become more determined to remove it. February 24, 1988 [the effective banning of opposition organizations] was a historical event because it got the church leaders to take a stand that they have never taken before.

The government created a crisis for the churches. The churches had been talking about nonviolence and peaceful change, and most of them had condemned violence. But now the church leaders felt we could no longer just talk about nonviolence; we needed to act. So we marched in Cape Town.

We have proved that today the road of nonviolence in South Africa is very short. The system doesn't allow for nonviolent activity. I interpreted the government order of February 24 as saying to the victims of apartheid, "We can't handle you at the nonviolent political level, so we're closing all the doors; we want you at the military level."

Interestingly, Adriaan Vlok, the minister of law and order, said in Parliament, "These organizations realized that they couldn't match us at the military level. That's why they opted for what they call nonviolent mobilization of the masses to create a revolutionary situation." South Africa, in essence, opted for violence on the 24th of February. That's what created the crisis for the church leaders. So you needed to be honest enough to go and march.

I've talked about honest and dishonest nonviolent disciples. Dishonest nonviolent disciples use nonviolence to stop people from resisting the system. But honest nonviolent disciples want to see nonviolent protest working.

I was a bit worried when the decision was made on Thursday, February 25, for us to march; I felt that this could divide the Council of Churches. Now you can imagine what that means to the general secretary. But amazingly, the brutal act of the state united the church leaders and caused us to make a decision to do something we could never do before. We came out of the march more united than ever. I think we are going to broaden the ecumenical structure in South Africa more than white people ever thought.

Wallis: *Since the march, the air is full of accusations from the government against the churches. You have been at the center of much of this because of your letter to P. W. Botha [see pp. 156–58] and his now famous letter in response, which attacked the church leaders [see pp. 159–63.].*

Chikane: I suspect that the state is going to be forced to be more brutal against the church simply because of the amazing determination of church leaders. I suspect that the state might try other than just the legal methods of dealing with church leaders. We are already experiencing harassment and attacks. We might have to go through an experience of assassinations and people disappearing. I believe that the state is going to try to close this space for the church.

Wallis: *The state is saying the church leaders are not really church leaders, that the people will not follow them.*

Chikane: I don't think the state president has the credentials to decide whether we are church or not. They [government leaders] are used to the Dutch Reformed Church, which blesses the state, so when you begin to question them, they say, "You are not the church."

You could see from the upsurge of support for the church leaders that we are going to get the body of Christ—the whole body, the congregations—taking up the issues themselves. I find it amazing that the churches in South Africa—at least those who are member churches of the Council—have moved away from debate about whether they can or should do anything as a church. They are debating what type of action they need to take.

The attacks on the church by the state have, in fact, mobilized more Christians. This mobilization that P. W. has caused is amazing. The government will have to face a massive upsurge of the members of the churches against the apartheid system. Anything they do besides going to the negotiating table is going to make the situation worse.

Wallis: *What will happen when honest, nonviolent disciples take their place in the streets, willing to put their lives on the line against a system that has demonstrated its willingness to be so vicious and brutal? What is ahead for the church and the country in this period?*

Chikane: I think we've entered the worst period, and it's going to become much worse than it is at the present moment. I suspect that as the congregations go to the streets, the system is going to be more and more brutal. And it's going to mean the murder of a lot of our people. And in the course of the murder of our people, the system will begin to disintegrate because of the contradictions created by its own brutality.

It seems—and this is a painful thing—that the international community does not respond unless we die in great numbers. When we want to take on the system, some say, "You're committing suicide, you know. You're going to be murdered." And we say, "Can you help us?" If they say, "No, we cannot help you," what they are telling us is to leave the system to oppress us indefinitely. So we find ourselves in a vulnerable situation where we cannot do otherwise but, in fact, offer ourselves for sacrifice.

I don't believe we as a church can now avoid the cross. If Jesus Christ had an option, I would think he would not have gone to the cross. One theologian said, "Jesus Christ didn't choose to die. He simply had no option but to die."

And it looks as though we have no option in the face of the level of evil in this country. For us to go over into victory, we will have to go through the cross.

Through that experience of the cross, I believe the system is going to be put down, and the church will come out being the real church of Christ. In this situation, if you're not a persecuted church, it seems that you can't become a real church of Christ.

Now we are faced with the reality that to be a Christian has to be a conscious decision. It is going to be too costly for those who became Christians by tradition or chance. Some might withdraw from the church. People will have to make very conscious decisions, knowing that to choose Christ is to choose death for the sake of justice against evil.

By going through that experience, we are forced to review our Christian faith, our own commitment. And that might be helpful in cleansing the church in South Africa. But I'm convinced that our victory is going to be at the level of that experience.

Wallis: *What can you say about the role of whites in this struggle?*

Chikane: A small number of whites have taken a stand against the apartheid system. And their presence in our midst helps us to lessen the type of pain people go through. If we could get many white Christians to come in, it would help to lessen the pain even more.

But I'm not very hopeful that this will happen. Those churches with whites in them would have to begin to preach the gospel in such a way that whites would have to choose whether they would stay in those churches. At the end we would have church members who would take a stand against the government which gives them the benefits.

Wallis: *Your situation seems to many on the outside to be hopeless. Yet I'm deeply amazed and moved, as you face the cross, by the hope that you and others express again and again.*

Chikane: I think one feels pessimistic when one approaches the problem from a pastoral perspective. As a pastor you're concerned about the lives of people, the pain they are going to go through. You wish that it wouldn't happen. It is just like Jesus saying, "I wish that this cup would pass." Humanly no one wants to go through that experience.

But on the other hand, it is that experience that gives you hope, because through that experience one has redemption, one has freedom. And because there's no option, we're bound as Christians to go through that experience.

Especially during 1986, as the system became more brutal, the young people said they actually felt they were closer to their liberation. They understand the fact that you cannot get closer to liberation without bringing out the viciousness of the system. The pain is an indication of the closeness to your day of liberation.

It is our faith that gives us hope. We know that in our helplessness we become more dependent on God. In our powerlessness we become powerful. It is our weakness that is our strength.

Those who run the evil system know it will end, and therefore they have no hope. They just become madder by the day, and in their madness take more and more lives. But we know that our struggle is a just one. That is really what makes it hopeful — God cannot allow evil to prevail forever.

Wallis: *One would hope that as you move toward the cross, the eyes and ears and hearts of the church all over the world would be awakened to respond.*

Chikane: Our act is redemptive — not in the sense that Christ died to redeem the world — but that, in our weakness, our experience helps other people to have a new understanding of their faith and their commitment. And so the suffering of the church in South Africa itself becomes a message of salvation and hope and redemption for the greater body of Christ.

"I believe that the church will not really confront the state until such time as the church has rediscovered itself."

7

A Struggle for the Church's Soul: Affirming the Gospel in South Africa

An Interview with Charles Villa-Vicencio

Charles Villa-Vicencio is head of the Department of Religious Studies at the University of Cape Town in South Africa. He was interviewed at the university.

Jim Wallis: *What are your impressions of the current status of the church-state conflict in South Africa?*

Charles Villa-Vicencio: I would certainly say that we are experiencing a church-state confrontation in the present situation. I would also want to introduce a word of caution with regards to this, inasmuch as there is not a direct confrontation between state per se and church per se.

What I'm pleading for is an understanding that when we talk about the church, we are not talking about a homogeneous group of people. The churches are divided. Every conceivable division that one discerns within society as a whole in this country one discerns within the life of the churches.

Second, there is, in fact, a yawning gap between the church

as it is — as a social institution — and the church as it theologically ought to be. It ought to be an agent of God. However, the church is not that in practice.

We recognize that this God who has called the church into being is a God who is decidedly on the side of the poor and the oppressed rather than the rich and the powerful. We recognize very clearly that the church is not where it ought to be. The church historically and institutionally in this country, since the time of its birth with the arrival of the missionaries in the nineteenth century, has been on the side of the status quo. There have been groups within the church who have sought to locate themselves on the side of the poor and the oppressed, but the church as institution has been on the side of the status quo.

The so-called English-speaking churches, meaning loosely those churches that belong to the South African Council of Churches, have a marvelous track record. They have protested consistently and persistently against apartheid and against the introduction of every conceivable new form of oppression over the years. In recent times they've even gone so far as to declare the government to be illegitimate.

These same churches, however, have failed when it comes to translating that protest into resistance. When it comes to translating their resolutions that have gone through synods and conferences and general assemblies into political programs, they are weak. The churches have protested without becoming an inherent part of the political struggle for the duration.

Institutionally, the churches have allowed themselves to be domesticated by the dominant forces within society. They've allowed themselves to be forced to live in a little ghetto, where the emphasis is on other-worldly theology rather than a theology that engages them in struggle.

The churches have accepted the formula which has been prescribed over the years by a succession of rulers, both within and without the church. It is a formula which says theology and politics don't mix. The church has suppressed and ignored that dimension of its own tradition which emphasized social engagement. It has been said that the best-kept secret in the theology of the church is that theology which requires the church to be engaged in social, political, and economic issues.

There is indeed a measure of truth—only a limited measure, but a measure of truth—in P. W. Botha's statement that leaders such as Allan Boesak, and Frank Chikane, and Desmond Tutu do not enjoy the support of all members of the churches. When he implies that they are not representative of the witness and character of the churches, he is right. They are ahead of the institutional churches. That is the right place for leaders to be— ahead of the constituency, pulling them forward.

Where P. W. Botha is wrong—and he's categorically wrong— is when he suggests that people like Boesak, Tutu, and Chikane are inspired by some extraneous Marxist doctrine, or they're receiving their instructions from the ANC [African National Congress]. I've never known Desmond Tutu to receive instructions from anybody except God.

The leaders are different not because their doctrine is different; they are different because they are authentically articulating a gospel which the church, in its better moments, knows it ought to articulate. They are standing within the mainstream and the main tradition of the theology of the church—that tradition and that theology upon which the institutional churches were originally based, but which have been left behind as domestication has taken hold.

What I perceive happening in South Africa is a conflict not only between church on the one hand and state on the other. I see a conflict within the church between those reactionary forces that continue to seek to domesticate the church and those forces within the church represented by people like Desmond Tutu and Allan Boesak and Frank Chikane, who, in fact, are affirming the radical gospel of Jesus Christ, which requires people to live in a certain way both spiritually and in terms of social action. It is a struggle, in other words, for the soul of the church.

It's very important for us to ask, if Tutu and Boesak and Chikane do not represent the entire church, why is it that they are perceived as such a significant danger to the status quo and to the state? P. W. Botha is absolutely right. He's not having bad dreams; he's right—they are a danger to the state. Why? For three reasons.

First, they are articulating a message that is instinctively understood and responded to by the majority of the oppressed people, who make up the majority of the church. They recognize that message to be the message of the residual gospel of liberation which has been suppressed for so long within the life of the church.

It's the gospel they read about in the New Testament, even if it's not proclaimed in their pulpits. They know it is the gospel of Jesus Christ, and they respond instinctively to it. P. W. Botha — when he hears those people preach, and when he notes the response — must have, and ought to have, sleepless nights.

Second, what we are experiencing within the life of the church today is an organization, a mobilization, of the church of the poor and the oppressed in a way that we've never seen before. As I look back on the history of the church in this country, this is the first time that there is an overt and explicit attempt by significant and recognized church leaders to mobilize the poor and the oppressed within the churches to be on the side of the broad liberation struggle.

Third, for the first time in the history of this church, we have seen a new breed of church leadership emerge — a breed of leadership which is representative of the majority who are oppressed. A breed of leadership who articulate the values, the aspirations, the hopes and the fears, the determination, and the commitment of the oppressed.

That is a significant shift. That is where my hope lies for the church — that we have leaders articulating a message that is understood to be the gospel. We are seeing through their urgency, and the urgency of others, the mobilization of the poor within the church. We are seeing a group in leadership who are prepared to act ecumenically and corporately to oppose the state. That is good news, no question about it.

What, then, is the confrontation? I would say the confrontation is between the state and that group within the church who are seeking to affirm the radical gospel of Jesus Christ — that residual gospel which has been suppressed, which has been covered by layers of piety and all kinds of other theology to the point that it's hardly recognizable.

That gospel, sometimes referred to as a dangerous memory within the church that is being reawakened within this period of time, is being rearticulated by these people. Thus the church, as institution, is not very well-equipped to deal with this new phase of renewal. The people within the church who are oppressed are beginning to rise up almost instinctively, and certainly passionately, in response to this articulation of the gospel. It constitutes the hope of the church.

As we see this initiative to organize and mobilize the church of the poor—and it is a significant threat to the state—we would be very, very wrong if we for one moment forgot that the forces of oppression within this country are going to act to counter that move. They are going to act not only through the intensification of repression and oppression, but also by seeking to counter it through right-wing movements within the church, by spending a great deal of money there.

We ought also to recognize that this process of transformation, this process of renewal which we are witnessing within the life of the church, is a process that has come about as a result of forces very often outside of the church, as a result of the broad liberation struggle within the country spilling back into the church. These extra-parliamentary groups outside of the church are now restricted; so people are looking to the church to engage themselves, as a vehicle through which to pursue the struggle.

That's not bad news, or a misuse of the church. It's good news. The church is offering a home to the poor and the oppressed, which is a basic message of the New Testament. As oppression is penetrating the life of the church, so the world, interestingly enough, is reactivating within the church a latent and almost forgotten gospel of resistance and commitment to a totally transformed social order. That is what I see happening in South Africa; the struggle is on.

Wallis: *Are the poor and oppressed whom you refer to within the churches, or are most outside of the churches?*

Villa-Vicencio: Black people in this country constitute about 85 percent of the population. Therefore, almost by definition, probably a minimum of 85 percent of the churches are black. Given the socio-economic structure of this country, the majority of black people are poor and oppressed. When one talks about the church of the poor and oppressed, one is talking about the majority of people who have some allegiance to the church.

When we talk about the life of the church, we are talking about different constituencies. The white Dutch Reformed Church is a large church with a large number of whites. And although they are a minority, significant groups of white people within the so-called English-speaking, SACC-member churches carry a fair amount of clout economically and otherwise.

Transformation and change do not come about merely by dreaming great dreams, but also by doing hard analysis. We'd be making a fundamental mistake if we did not remind ourselves that the largest segment of the black church in this country is the African independent churches. Many are trapped within very top-heavy types of hierarchial theology, but there are signs of very real renewal and transformation taking place in those churches.

Wallis: *Is the church making any headway in the black townships? How do the comrades and the youth feel about the churches?*

Villa-Vicencio: The impression I get as I speak with people in the townships is that many of these people in recent years drifted out of the churches. They turned their backs on the institutional churches per se, because what they experienced happening in those churches was totally divorced from, and indifferent to, what was happening in the world of their daily lives. They "voted with their feet" — an expression I think Americans have used. They left.

What one has seen in recent days, as the church has taken a more explicit stand, is that many of these comrades are looking at the church and saying, "Hey! What's going on here?" They are beginning to see that the church is not that homogeneous group on the side of the status quo. If they look carefully, they discern a struggle for the life of the church, and they begin to show interest.

We go into the townships to pray for the downfall of the government. I've often said to my colleagues in these situations, "I would love to do a census right here to determine how many of these people go to church on Sunday."

The comrades, and others who are opposed to the system and struggling to transform it, are very excited. They are interested, at least, in what is happening in this alternative church. It is to those issues that the comrades respond, not necessarily to the institutional churches. We would be wrong if we overestimated the influence of the institutional church.

Wallis: *You have spoken of the domesticated church that has lost the memory of the gospel. There is another church in this land, which has been more than domesticated; it has been the bulwark, the theological justifier, of the state. What is the role of the Dutch Reformed Church in the current situation?*

Villa-Vicencio: I have never for one moment thought that the white Dutch Reformed churches were in the process of undergoing change. The Dutch Reformed Church now talks the language of P. W. Botha, and so-called reformism and pragmatism. But the fundamentals are exactly the same as they always were. These guys have now been revealed for who they are and where they are: firmly on the side of, and in the pocket of, the government.

It's a little difficult to discern whether they in fact control the government, or whether the government controls them; but they are hand in glove. There's no question about it. No question about it whatsoever.

What frightens me, when it comes to looking at some of the statements that are made by some of the leaders of the white Dutch Reformed Church, is that there are far too many liberal church leaders in this country who actually get taken in by them. Our analysis has to be far, far better than that. We've got to be as wise as serpents; otherwise, we are going to be misled.

Wallis: *When P. W. Botha writes a letter attacking the church leaders, the letter is replete with theological language, biblical quotations, references to Jesus, and religious challenges. Does the state president have the theological capacity to write those letters himself, or does he have advisers writing his letters for him or with him?*

Villa-Vicencio: I have absolutely no doubt in my mind that P. W. Botha is incapable of writing those letters and many things that he says in them. Just who those unknown scribes are, I don't know.

Wallis: *"Scribes" is an interesting word to use for them.*

Villa-Vicencio: Indeed. There are rumors as to who was, in fact, advising the prosecution in the [government's] Eloff Commission inquiry into the SACC. Certainly the position that the Eloff Commission ultimately came out with was more or less the position that was adopted by Johan Heyns, the moderator of the

Dutch Reformed Church, in his submission to the Eloff Commission. There is a very cozy relationship there. There's absolutely no question about it.

We listen to President Botha's attacks on the church. They are the words of a very angry, bad-tempered old man. We all know that Botha has a very bad temper; I think we should just ignore it. I think we should talk about the mandate of the church—to be obedient to the gospel of Jesus Christ.

Wallis: *It's as if there's a church that is not only in the pocket of the state, but is almost synonymous with the state. The state president boasts about his being a Christian and a member of the Dutch Reformed Church. And so you have the state claiming a primary sort of ecclesial legitimacy over and against those who would challenge the state.*

Then you have the church that you call the liberal church, which has protested but has not resisted. And the church which you are calling the alternative church, which is taking the lead and now includes the institutional leaders, in many cases, of at least the English-speaking churches. So this church is expanding and moving into more places. If what the church leaders are talking about and hoping for—a mobilization in the streets of the masses of Christians from many churches—comes to be, do you think the state will treat that response any differently than it has treated various challenges to its power before?

Villa-Vicencio: Contrary to what P. W. Botha has said, I would find it hard to accept that the strategists in the government could be counseling the government to go for the confrontation between church and state. I don't think it's in the interest of the state.

If the churches begin to be a vehicle for mobilizing the poor and the oppressed in resistance against the system—if the churches begin to become a threat to the security of the state—I have no doubt that the state will act against them in the most ruthless way possible. They will do it in such a way as to try to convince large sections of the white community in this country that this is not the church per se, because what happens in the church is what happens on a Sunday morning inside a church building.

To them, when people take to the streets, we're no longer

talking about Christian worship. We're now talking about something else. They will say to the white populace that the communists are using the church for devious ends. They will act against it in the most gruesome way.

It is very difficult for the state to act against the obvious leaders such as Boesak and Tutu and Chikane. That must be a headache for them. If they try to formally restrict any of them, I have no doubt that those people would believe that, in obedience to God, they are obliged to disobey those restrictions.

If they put them in prison, if they detain them, there's going to be a major uprising. So what happens then? How do they get rid of them? I don't know. I'm not suggesting anything. All I want to say is that other prominent leaders within this country have disappeared; they have encountered their death in a very mysterious way. At whose hands? Through what agencies? I don't know.

But I don't think it is an overstatement when we read in the newspaper that Allan Boesak fears assassination. There are enough cranks running around. There are enough right-wing agencies that would be ready and willing to do it.

Wallis: *So for the church to rediscover the dangerous memory of the gospel in South Africa, it needs to enter into not only a period of confrontation between church and state, but also into the experience of suffering on the part of the people of God?*

Villa-Vicencio: I believe that the church will not really confront the state until such time as the church has rediscovered itself. Judgment begins with the household of God. We have got to discover what it means to be a church not only in solidarity with the poor, but a church *of* the poor — allowing, enabling, and empowering the poor to take control of the church and to be the church, giving it identity, giving it a program, and giving it direction. That's the challenge facing the churches.

It is important for church leaders to march. We will all march from time to time. Yet, more important is for the church to go into Crossroads, to go into the squatter camps, and to be a part of the poor and the oppressed in the sense of empowering the poor and the oppressed.

If the confrontation between church and state is going to happen, let it happen there. Let the state move in and prevent us from being the church when we are about God's business of uplifting the poor and the oppressed. That is a costly presence.

Wallis: *If the church does respond, it will suffer. What do you as an African church person have to say to the church in the United States and elsewhere? What kind of solidarity, what kind of symbolic and concrete support, are going to be required in this period?*

Villa-Vicencio: Solidarity is very important. When you are sitting in prison, when you are being convinced by your interrogators that you've been forgotten, and then you come out and know that there were a whole lot of Christians both at home and abroad doing what they could to support you, and to support your family, that's very important. Don't let anybody ever underestimate the importance of simple support and solidarity.

Second, there are a number of programs in which we are engaged in this country, in which the churches are deeply involved both here and abroad—the disinvestment campaign, pressure on embassies, especially of Western governments. In that area, many of the churches have been very responsive. And also in the area of providing needed funds and resources.

When you say to me, "What about the churches in the United States or anywhere else?" I would want to say to my sisters and my brothers over there—and this is the most important point— that you have to discover what it means to be the church of the poor and the oppressed in your own country. When I look at the socio-economic and racial divisions in churches in this country, and then I go abroad and visit your country, I've got a strange, uneasy feeling that I'm right at home. That's what disturbs me. I don't think that Christians in the United States or in other parts of the world are really in a position to minister to us until they have dealt with the fundamental issues of racism and economic injustice within their own countries.

One of the major reasons why the present regime in South Africa continues to exist is because of the good services rendered to this regime by the United States. We are what we are— we have the resources we have—because the multinationals in your country sustain our economy, and develop our economy, and get rich off our economy. Until the churches take on those demonic forces within your country, those churches aren't really coming to grips with the issue of this country. If Christians in your country are going to live with all the comforts and all the prosperities of a Western capitalist, so-called free enterprise First World nation, one that oppresses Third World nations, and at the same time make nice liberal noises about suffering in South Africa, then I get the impression that they are making those noises to ease their own consciences rather than addressing the fundamental problem that we have in this country. That's the way I see it.

The division that you have in the world between a First World nation, such as the United States, and Third World nations, you also have in Washington, D.C., and New York. The division between First World and Third World nations is what we are experiencing in South Africa.

What one can witness in South Africa is not some sort of strange society, an aberration. It is in fact a microcosm of what is happening globally. As First World nations are wealthy and prosperous as a result of the poverty of Third World nations, so it is in South Africa. We have one nation—mainly the wealth of the whites, the wealth of the establishment—that is a direct consequence of the poverty and oppression of blacks in the country.

We are seeing here in a very explicit and grotesque way—a diabolical way—what the world is experiencing in a less obvious, less explicit, and less concentrated way. But that does not make it any less evil in other places.

I think we should be saying to Christians around the world that we all need to join the struggle. We need to disturb you, you need to disturb us. In solving your problem, you will help us solve ours. We need to join together globally in transforming the social and economic order.

"God knows the powerfulness of women. That is why when Jesus Christ had to be born Mary did it alone, without the help of Joseph. The Christian faith liberates women. But we have refused to be liberated."

8

We Carry the Cross Close to Us: Theology for the Struggle

An Interview with Motlalepula Chabaku

Motlalepula Chabaku, a pastor in exile from South Africa, was interviewed by Joyce Hollyday, associate editor of Sojourners.

Joyce Hollyday: *You have been an outspoken opponent of apartheid for many years. How has your background prepared you for this task?*

Motlalepula Chabaku: I was born in Johannesburg, South Africa, in the month of November, a peak spring month. Suddenly, there was thunder, lightning, torrential rain, and I came. My parents gave me the name Motlalepula, which means "One who comes with the rain."

My parents believed that God timed my coming into the world for a special purpose. Even though I may be critical of issues, acting like thunder and lightning, I must be like the rain. In our part of the world, rain is a very scarce commodity. We look forward to it, because where there is rain, there is water;

where there is water, there is life; where there is life, there is growth, re-creation, hope. And so I have to come with hope, even in a hopeless situation.

My parents could only afford to educate me up to the sixth grade. So I would pick up discarded exercise books which the whites received with their free and compulsory education, and use a razor blade to cut the empty pages and glue them together with a paste made from condensed milk. Then I sold them to pay for my school fees after sixth grade.

I never took no for an answer. Every problem that came to me was not a problem but a challenge. If I am made in God's image, no human being can put me down. This has been my conviction. It was tough, but I went on.

The Episcopal churches of South Africa offered me a scholarship, and I was trained as a teacher. I taught a class of eighty children. Although education for blacks is inferior, I refused to accept this. I got white children to come to the black school for one day. And the black and white children felt the oneness; they wanted to be friends; they learned phrases in each other's languages. It was hope in a hopeless situation.

Hollyday: *How have being a Christian, and being a South African woman, shaped your perspective?*

Chabaku: For me to be a Christian means to be a member of the body of Christ with all human beings. If you are one body and any part of the body suffers, you feel the pain, and you react. I could not keep quiet when there was injustice.

There are a lot of people who have a false notion that to be Christian is to be pious, sanctimonious, unquestioning, like an ingrown toenail. But to be a Christian is to continue changing lives, and structures of society; and if you don't change people and structures, you are sinning.

I am a woman. I am part of that global force of people who are despised, deprived, discriminated against, and yet we form more than half of the world's population.

In South Africa, we have a law that makes all black women minors for life. I can't even sign my own documents; I have to get a sixteen-year-old boy to give me consent to apply for a travel document. I cannot lodge a complaint in a police station because I am a minor—a man has to complain for me. These laws are passed by a government that is 90 percent Christian, with the support of the Western world that is predominantly Christian.

The black woman bears the worst of the brunt of oppression in South Africa. Women are not allowed to join their husbands in the cities and can only see their husbands, and sometimes their children, for three weeks or a month a year. We are the lowest paid people.

I defied many laws in South Africa. As a single woman I was not allowed to have a house. I harangued, cajoled, and finally got a house in my name. They said a single woman could not adopt children. I battled and adopted my daughter, Mamolemo.

I take my vision and courage from nature, from water. There is a poem about the brook. When water wants to go downstream it doesn't matter how many boulders you put in there. It will circumvent the rocks. You may delay it, but you can never stop it moving. And so we may have to change our strategies, but never our commitment.

When the government issued passbooks to women, I tell you, we moved heaven and earth. My job as secretary of the African National Congress was to organize a protest against them. Passbooks are not passports or travel documents. They have destroyed more lives and separated more families in South Africa than any other thing.

When the African National Congress was outlawed, the ideas were not outlawed in my heart. You can ban an organization, but you cannot destroy it in the hearts of the people.

I am concerned about the rights of women, the rights of children, and just as equally, the rights of men; because there can never be a community, there can never be a family, there can never be true freedom when any sector of humanity is not free.

We women have the special role of working for peace and liberation because we have a great power for peace. It was a woman like Harriet Tubman who was able to liberate men, women, and children. It was a woman like Rosa Parks who turned the tide of history. Women can be a source of hope and peace, if we rise and play the responsible role to which we are called. Jesus called us specially, specially.

God respects women. God knows the powerfulness of women. That is why when Jesus Christ had to be born Mary did it alone, without the help of Joseph. The Christian faith liberates women. But we have refused to be liberated.

When it was lawful and traditional for a prostitute to be stoned to death, Jesus spoke for the prostitute. Jesus at that time was not concerned about her sin, but about her life.

Jesus gave the woman freedom—but not just freedom. It was freedom with responsibility.

Jesus Christ ventured out with women. The women were the first people to bring the good news that Jesus had risen. The first. The men thought the women were mad or drunk.

When Jesus Christ was put on the cross, we don't hear about the twelve disciples. They were not there. When Christ was removed from the cross, in that thunder and in that storm, it was women who were wailing over that body. And when that body was taken to the grave, it was the women who ventured to say they would buy spices to go and embalm the body, even though it was dangerous to be identified with the body of a criminal.

Where were the disciples? They were scared. They were feeling leaderless, voiceless, because Jesus was not there. Why then are we women remaining behind? What's our excuse? Why have we left the men to carry the responsibility alone in the churches, to be the decision makers?

We as Christian women have to deal with the total person, affected by religious, political, economic, and social factors. You find politics in the Bible from the first page to the last. Jesus Christ himself was political, and so people who say we are not supposed to be involved in politics may not have a full understanding of the Gospels and of the word "evangelical." What does it mean? It means someone who brings a message; we have to be bearers of good news.

Hollyday: *You have suffered greatly, and now you live in exile from your home. What keeps you speaking out against apartheid?*

Chabaku: I know that my sharing honestly about the investments in South Africa which exploit my people is seen by the South African government as tantamount to economic sabotage, which is punishable by death. But we are called as Christians to be on the side of justice, of honesty, and pay the price for it. I have known police beatings and interrogations.

My heart and mind and roots are in South Africa, and I want

to go back. But I don't know whether it is helpful to go back and face a gun, because when you are a corpse you are newsworthy for one week and then you are no longer helpful. I also wonder how effective I would be if I were in jail.

In South Africa, the gold mines are owned by a company called the Anglo-American Corporation—English and American cooperating. We see the price of gold going up when we are not shareholders of the gold in our motherland. Approximately 65 percent of the businesses in South Africa are owned by outsiders.

If you were an American and the Soviet Union came in and took over your resources and employed you to mine them, wouldn't you feel like saying, "Get out, Russia!"? But when you say so, then the whole world says to you, "You must be grateful that Russia came here and provided jobs."

That same stupid argument has been used in our motherland. We never invited Europeans to come to our country. They saw the wealth and strategic position of our country. And they took advantage of our ignorance.

Many businesses in South Africa are exploiting us. For years we have been suffering but trying to say, yes, even though the land is ours, let's share it. But nobody listened to us. Now that there is pressure from inside and outside, suddenly these companies are talking about our plight. They say that if they move out, we will suffer.

We have always suffered. If there are withdrawals of investment in South Africa, yes, the Africans will suffer. But whites will suffer most, because they have the highest wages, benefits, and privileges.

For instance, a white will get paid one hundred dollars a week for the same job I do, and I get five dollars a week. If the company withdraws, who loses most? But you start saying, "How will she survive without the five dollars?"

In South Africa black employees cannot say, "I am tired," or "I am sick," or "I'm resigning." The employer has the right to arrest you and take you to jail for leaving your job. Blacks are not allowed to belong to trade unions with whites, and the few black trade unions do not have the same legal bargaining power as the white unions.

A number of products have been declared illegal in America because they are dangerous to health. These products are sold in South Africa. You have your Depo-Provera pill, used for birth control. It causes cancer and internal bleeding. It's being pushed in black communities by the government of South Africa and many companies. Why? Because whites in South Africa want South Africa to be white South Africa. They are basing their desire on American history.

The European whites in America have basically gotten rid of the indigenous Native American people. White South Africans have exactly the same picture. It's the same idea as when you set up your Indian reservations. "Homelands" are being set up in South Africa, which are reservations for blacks. Same idea, same background, same history, same racism, same people.

Hollyday: *What do you see for the future of South Africa? And what role can concerned Christians in the United States play?*

Chabaku: South Africa is the last bastion of white capitalism and white domination. As our God has been liberating the whole of Africa, most of the reactionary whites have been going south. When Angola became independent, the reactionary whites and Portuguese went to South Africa. When Mozambique and Kenya became independent, they went to South Africa. Zimbabwe has now become independent. Where are the whites going? South Africa.

Where else will they go after South Africa? Because our country is going to be free, too. It is going to be a nonracial society. They can only go to the sea. So they are going to fight until the blood comes up to the stirrups.

When we blacks, who have been voteless, voiceless, landless in our motherland, have tried peaceful changes, we have been met with violence. More and more, people see that violence is the only answer. I belong to those who still hope for peaceful change in the midst of escalating violence.

As Christians we are called to give life, give liberation. People are getting disillusioned with the Christian faith, the Western world, and capitalism. They're not against the Christian faith as such, but they're against how it has been misused, misunderstood, exploited. A knife is a very good utensil in the house, but if you take it and stab people with it, it doesn't mean that the knife is bad, it is the people who have misused the knife. The Christian faith is very liberating. But the Christian faith has been misused.

So when my brothers and sisters go for an armed struggle, I cannot condemn them. I know many peace-loving people who have been forced into violence. They have suffered violence, and in desperation they turn to counterviolence. And we always blame the oppressed when they take up arms; we don't blame the oppressor.

If you want to help us in South Africa, deal with the oppressors. They have the power. They are the source of all the terror.

And what does the United States do? It believes in human rights, but it supports brutal regimes and dictatorships all over the world. Somoza was the best friend of the United States, not of the Nicaraguans. The United States is a friend of Pinochet, not of the Chileans. The Shah was a friend of the United States, not the Iranians.

The majority of Americans are very loving, caring, trusting people, who really don't care for violence. But your major policies give a false picture of the United States.

Look at the record of the United States in the United Nations. The United States condemns South Africa and says its policies are wrong, but when it comes to action, the U.S. government goes only three ways: It abstains, it opposes, or it vetoes. The United States makes it impossible for any action to be implemented on South Africa.

And who makes the decisions for you? It is your business houses. They have employed lobbyists who influence your decisions, and it is those decisions that prevail, not those of the ordinary voter.

The United States has laws that are destroying life. Look at the story of David and Goliath. David's family was suffering from hunger as they were on the battlefield. He used to bring food to them. But that did not decrease the number of casualties they suffered. It was only when David began to deal with the main source of terror and violence, which was Goliath, that there was no more need to send food.

This is one of the problems of the church; it tends to concentrate on relief programs. When Jesus Christ healed the poor, the sick, and the hungry, he was liberating them from charity. They were dependent on alms, on whatever they could beg. But Jesus Christ gave them back their humanity, so they could have life, and have it in abundance.

The church in the Western world is so steeped in materialism, in structure, that it loses people. Meanwhile, Christ is being hurt and is crying in pain in places of hunger and torture. Christ is alive in areas of conflict, but where people are materially comfortable, they find it difficult to carry the cross of Christ. They have their house first, the insurance, their car, family, and after all this, they have the cross. How can they hold it with all that too?

We have nothing. We carry the cross close to us. That's why we find Christians growing in number in areas of strife and conflict: Latin America, Africa, and Asia.

And we have something to give the Western world, we who come from those areas that are labelled "Third World." God made no mistake by spreading around the gifts that we need, so we can learn to share.

Johannesburg. 1 June 1987. Delegates from women's organizations throughout South Africa gather to discuss the rebirth of the Federation of South African women which was active in the 1950s.

"We must open our hearts and our minds, our whole beings to others' needs, and absorb and allow the Spirit of God to interpret to us what is happening and what should be our message and our response. In that sense it is a process of continuous conversion of our whole lives. . . ."

9

To Love When Others Hate:
A Journey of Obedience
to God

An Interview with
Beyers Naudé

---

*Beyers Naudé was the youngest person ever to join the Broeder
bond, the secret Afrikaner society that conceived apartheid, of
which his father was a founder. He became a pastor in the
Dutch Reformed Church; but in 1963 he severed his ties with
that church because of his anti-apartheid beliefs. He later
served as the general secretary of the South African Council
of Churches. He was interviewed by Jim Wallis in Washington,
D.C.*

Jim Wallis: *I'm greatly intrigued by your conversion, because
conversion is the core of our Christian faith. Many of us in the
United States are on the journey of conversion. There's so much
from your history that bears upon ours and that helps shed light on
our experience.*

*You have talked about how you finally had to go see for yourself
the situation of black people in South Africa. And then, of course,
you speak of the Sharpeville Massacre. I was particulary intrigued*

*by your response when asked sometime ago about your conversion —
how and why it happened and what was behind it. You said, "I
read the Bible. That's all."*

Beyers Naudé: I think I should start by saying that I am an
Afrikaner, born in a deeply religious Afrikaner home that was
very conservative politically, with a father who fought in the
Anglo-Boer War on the side of the Boers and who deeply loved
the Afrikaner people.

After four years of academic study, I continued with four
years of theological study. During all those years, the question
of apartheid being biblically unjustifiable never arose. Apartheid
was simply taken for granted: The Bible supported apartheid,
the Bible blessed it, and the Bible sanctioned it. And I never
questioned this in any way critically, because I'd assumed that
it was something that had been properly thought through.

I served a number of white congregations in South Africa
until 1949, when I was called to become what you call here a
"university chaplain" of the Dutch Reformed Church at Pretoria
University. During that period I began to look at what was happening in Africa and realized that the period after the Second
World War, with decolonization taking place in the vast continent of Africa, would deeply affect the life of the Christian
churches, especially of the Dutch Reformed churches.

In the course of that thinking, the questions arose about
apartheid, and voices of dissent and rejection of apartheid in-
creased on the part of other churches, especially in South Africa.
So eventually I decided that I would undertake a self-study on
the biblical justification for apartheid, which I did between 1955
and 1957.

I came to the conclusion that my own church's attempt at
justifying apartheid on biblical grounds was simply not tenable.
Although it may have been sincerely intended, in fact it had no
proper, valid, biblical, or theological grounds. And for me that
was a shattering discovery, because the whole moral basis of
ministry with regard to the apartheid relationship between
whites and blacks was removed. That was the first experience,
or the first phase, in the process of conversion.

Wallis: *How is it that a church that no doubt prides itself on its
biblical fidelity did not ask in a biblical way a question about some-*

thing as fundamental as apartheid in South Africa? And how is it that you began to ask that question, when probably no one else around you did? I imagine that the more you asked the question, the more troublesome the question became.

Naudé: I think it came about because of the fact that the Afrikaners were of a deeply religious background. They simply took for granted the belief that in a special way they were a part of the elect nation of God. They believed they were called upon to evangelize and Christianize the heathen community of South Africa. They believed they had a divine mission and a divine charge given by God.

But because of the outlook of the Afrikaner people—their understanding of their divine calling and their deep-rooted, unconscious prejudices toward people of color—they did not realize to what degree they were deliberately or unconsciously distorting passages of the Bible simply to fit with their political and ideological or their racial outlook. And with church leadership giving full justification, with universities offering no critical approach, with the Afrikaner society being so totally isolated, it was very easy to present that ideology.

Wallis: *What happened in your life that led you to question whether the apartheid system was justifiable biblically?*

Naudé: The first thing was that I was mandated by the church in 1953, together with another minister, to undertake a study tour of church youth work. I was elected as the first chair of a national church youth society, which I was instrumental in forming. We undertook a six-and-a-half-month intensive study tour through Europe, the United States, and Canada. A number of these questions about apartheid arose during that tour.

The second phase of my conversion was during the period I was acting moderator of the Transvaal Synod. A number of young white ministers who were serving black congregations— that means congregations of Africans, Indians, and those people of mixed descent called "colored" in South Africa—were confronted by members of the different congregations. In the suffering that they were experiencing as a result of apartheid, they challenged the ministers, asking, "How can you justify this suffering on the basis of the gospel? What kind of a faith is this?"

The ministers called me in because of their deep concern and asked for advice. My first response to them was, "I can't believe what you are telling me is happening," because I was living in a happy, white, privileged ghetto of Afrikaner life in South Africa. When eventually I got the opportunity, I went out of my way to visit the parishes, the areas concerned. I discovered for the first time in my life what was happening, and I was shattered! To discover what apartheid was doing to human beings created in me a tremendous moral crisis.

The third and final phase was the event of the Sharpeville Massacre on March 21, 1960, when sixty-nine people who were protesting peacefully were simply shot, most of them in the back as they were running away. That was a moment in my life when I just felt I could not allow this situation to continue any longer.

Wallis: *I've read your testimony in several places, where you said, "I just had to see for myself. I had to go where I'd never been before. And just seeing it was a shattering experience." Here in Washington, D.C., most people who come to this hotel won't travel the few blocks necessary to see what is happening to poor people or the black underclass in the "shadows" of this city. It's really not deliberate in most cases; it's just that most people have never had the occasion to cross the barriers and boundaries that circumscribe their lives.*

Your experience raises the question, not just in South Africa but here or anywhere, of whether we can even understand the meaning of our faith if we can't break through those barriers.

Naudé: I fully agree. The problem in my country is that the church in the past has made a very serious mistake by presenting the Christian faith as primarily a rational belief based on a certain theological or theoretical understanding and interpretation of the gospel. Another mistake was not realizing that faith is meaningless unless it becomes contextualized.

If you talk about hunger, go and see where hunger is. If you talk about injustice, go and view what kind of injustice. If you talk about human dignity, go and see where human dignity is being violated. If you talk about racial prejudice, go and meet with the people who know themselves and experience themselves to be the victims of that prejudice.

Unless you are willing to do that, you can never discover the full truth of the gospel. That was the example of Jesus himself. But it's much easier to sit in your study and to preach about it.

Or to be in your theological school and theologize about it. Or to have academic, theoretical discussions and even write a book about it.

Dare yourself to be challenged by a faith that is real. Then go out into the highways and byways and say, "I want to be there when it happens. I want this to be part of my whole understanding of the Christian life and its challenge." But it's painful, because once you've set your foot on that new road it is a continuous process of conversion.

What makes that road so threatening to many people is that you never know where God is going to lead you next, what new challenge lies ahead, what new sacrifice, what new problems may arise. How will your Christian faith be able to meet that? To what degree does this require a greater form of sacrifice from yourself and your family? I suppose all of us are afraid to go that way, because we don't know the cost of going along that road.

Wallis: *There is a place in South African society, as there is in the United States, for a kind of liberal position or stance that is concerned and aware. But you have broken through that, in a way most whites in South Africa haven't, and indeed as most white people in this country haven't yet either, to a radical stance. How do you stay on this road and not get diverted to a liberal position, if you will, of observing the conflict and being a voice of reason and not really going where you need to go or taking sides with the people who are in fact really suffering?*

Naudé: I don't know what happens to other people. I can only describe what happened in my own life. First of all, I felt that if I wanted to commit myself to the truth, and therefore to an expression of the real love of Christ toward all human beings, I had to make myself open to others' feelings, concerns, pains, suffering, and joy. In order to do that, I had to set aside the time in order to make myself available to them, to move into where they are.

We must open our hearts and our minds and our whole beings to others' needs, and absorb and allow the Spirit of God to interpret to us what is happening and what should be our message and our response. In that sense it is a process of continuous

conversion of our own lives, and also of a deepening commitment all the time.

And what is helpful is if we specifically request those who
suffer to challenge us and to indicate to us where they feel that
our understanding is incomplete, where they feel that our commitment is not real or sincere, and where they feel more is
demanded. It is the moment that we become willing to open
ourselves to them, and therefore enable them to assist us, that
there is growth. It's the spiritual and the political and the social
growth and understanding that are required.

But if you're not prepared to do that—out of fear that it may
cost too much, the sacrifice may be too great, and the dangers
could be very, very serious—then that process of growth is
stalled. It does not go any further.

Wallis: *That's when we become stuck in a rut, or a position, or
a career that we maintain. But when we've stepped off or detoured
from that road, then we can be on a path to a deeper involvement
with suffering people.*

Naudé: That is true. But that is where the question of material
security plays a very important role, because you can feel that
there is so much at stake. From the viewpoint of material privilege and security, you find it becomes much more difficult to
even risk the possible loss of these things.

But if you know there is very little to lose, because whatever
you have you have committed to God, then you can say, "Well,
it's not mine. I share this with whomever may wish to have this."
Then there is an inner freedom that comes about as a result.
There is also, therefore, a liberty that you experience of being
available to people in their need. That's a tremendously enriching experience.

Wallis: The Observer, *a British newspaper, said in 1984 that
yours was "the longest journey of any South African of any colour,"
from where you came from to where you are now. People have said
of you, "He could have been the prime minister of South Africa."
But instead, you were banned for seven years. All that you gave up,
all that you've sacrificed, all that you could have had but have
turned away from—yet, you are not a person who acts as if you
have sacrificed or lost the great things in life. It seems that you have
gained, somehow, more than you've lost.*

Naudé: Oh, there's no doubt about it! What I've gained is so much more. I would never exchange this for all the positions in the world, all the possible situations of popularity that I would have had in South Africa. There's no question about it. I've gained an inner freedom and an inner peace of mind. I've also gained the ability to continue to love when others hate, to forgive when others would wish to enter into a situation of revenge.

Because of my experience, I've been able to tell other white Afrikaners, who despise me or have rejected me and feel that I'm a traitor to their cause, "I pity you, because I feel that you, in fact, have become the victims of your own imprisoned philosophy of life. And therefore you cannot be free. You cannot be free to love people of color deeply and sincerely. You cannot be free to look at the future of South Africa outside the confines of your present political viewpoint. You cannot be free to think of a church that operates in a totally different way. You cannot be open to the concept of Christian community with Christians of all denominations around the world. And therefore, as a result of those things that you have imposed on yourself, your vision is limited."

Wallis: *But there is a cost. I have a feeling that one painful place in your heart must be how much love you have for the church of your birth—a church that has so lost its way that it's labeled you traitor and heretic and worse. A break with the church is not painful if one doesn't love the church, but if one does, it's always a painful thing.*

Naudé: That is true. I think that was the most painful decision I had to make—to terminate my membership with the white Dutch Reformed Church. But the moment had to come when I made the decision and eventually said, "I'm sorry. I cannot, with a truthful conscience, remain a member of this church any longer." I can only hope that the day will come when the Dutch Reformed Church will understand and will realize that my motivation was one of deep concern and love for a church which, to my mind, has betrayed the essential calling of being the church of Christ.

Wallis: *Your decision was also hard for your family. But you and your wife have shared in this journey through it all. That must be a source of joy as well.*

Naudé: I continually thank God for the fact that my wife is able to stand with me, to go with me, even though at times it was very difficult for her to understand. And I also made a serious mistake in not interpreting to her, explaining to her, sharing with her enough of the inner tension and the problems which I foresaw coming to us. I wanted to spare and save her the agony and the pain, which is the wrong approach. I should have shared this with her much more deeply. But eventually, when we did do that, it became a tremendously enriching experience for both of us.

Wallis: *You are one of the most careful and insightful observers of South Africa today. Many in the United States have followed carefully and been deeply involved in the struggle and have seen the relationship between the struggle in South Africa and their own struggle here. How do you see that struggle now? What are the critical points, and what are the prospects? What are the connections between the struggle there and the struggle here?*

Naudé: First of all, it's important to emphasize that our situation in South Africa has entered a much more critical phase than the world outside realizes. Part of that is due to the fact that through the tremendous restrictions that have been placed on the media, the situation in South Africa is not known or appearing on the television screens of the world. And therefore people begin to believe that things are beginning to return to normal, which is definitely not the case.

The fact is that the oppression continues, though the emergency regulations are such that it seems as if, on the surface, it is quiet. But underneath is a ferment of anger, of bitterness, and of resistance occurring all the time. We've seen this with the restrictions imposed on the universities when the government demanded of the university councils that they should be the policing, or spying, agency of the church. There was a spontaneous reaction on the part of thousands of students who said, "We will not allow it."

Another example is the area of trade unions and workers, who are engaged in a very deep, serious, fundamental battle — a struggle for justice — for the workers of the country. A majority of the churches still don't understand the importance of this, its significance, and the effect it is going to have. So, my first point is that I think the situation is much more serious than we realize.

Second, we in South Africa have come to the conclusion that we will have to work out our liberation ourselves. We are very grateful for all the support which will come from outside; but we are also aware of the fact that, for instance, the governments of the United States, Great Britain, and the Federal Republic of Germany will make no meaningful contribution to our struggle for liberation. So, we have to find ways and means in order to bring about or speed up that process of liberation.

We are also realizing that the resistance will have to become much more serious. And, therefore, the danger of a conflict and a clash leading to bloodshed, violence, and even death is increasing. I think we simply have to prepare ourselves for a long and hard and painful struggle.

But the important point is that we should realize what basic moral, political, and economic issues are at stake. What is being tested in South Africa is, in fact, our whole value system, our concepts of justice, of love, of human concern.

The unwillingness of people in other parts of the world, including the United States, to confront similar challenges in their own societies makes our situation in South Africa much more difficult. But the moment we begin to see that there is a direct and a very meaningful link between the issues you are struggling with here and the issues in South Africa and Central America and the Middle East—that is the time we place our struggle in a wider perspective. And then it becomes meaningful.

Wallis: *What are the connections and links that you see?*

Naudé: First of all, as a Christian and an active member of the church, I feel that the churches of the different countries—all those religious leaders and religions that subscribe to the same spiritual and moral values that we subscribe to—must stretch out their hands. We must act in greater cooperation and unity in order to present this challenge to apartheid to the world.

Second, as churches and religious bodies, we must be more honest in admitting our own failures, in repenting for the fact that we could have done much more than we have done. We must challenge ourselves as Christian communities to be true to the deepest belief that we hold in our Christian faith.

Then it would be possible for us to begin to challenge the

secular communities, governments, and other organizations by saying, "We require a new vision. We require the understanding of a new world. We also require the understanding that God has made this world a kingdom for all people. We have enough to live in the world."

God, through creation, has given enough for every person in the world to survive. God gives us all the opportunities we need to develop ourselves out of the totality of our being and to build meaningful, responsible, sustainable societies—it is possible to do these things if we have the wisdom and the willingness to fulfill those opportunities and implement this vision. But the churches and the religious organizations have the major responsibility to offer that vision, to share that vision, and to make it a reality.

Wallis: *In the United States, people sometimes have difficulty understanding the relationship between the system of apartheid and our own system, or the global system under which apartheid exists. They say things like, "South Africa has a problem of racism now just like we had in the 1960s." The problem is not seen systemically by many people, and some people use apartheid's existence to focus energy on a problem "out there" rather than dealing with problems here. What are your systemic, theological reflections on this?*

Naudé: First of all, it's important to realize that the challenges to our faith and to our understanding of the responsibility that we have toward each other are basically the same, whether you deal with them in the United States or South Africa.

Certainly we have a racial problem, but we have much more than a racial problem. We've got a problem of social justice; we've got a problem of different classes; we've got a problem of some people living on a First World standard and some on a Third World standard; we've got a problem of wealth and poverty; we've got a problem of a much higher and a much lower quality of education being given to different people.

So basically it is a problem of what we are willing to do and how far we are willing to go to share our lives, our opportunities, and our privileges with those who don't have those things. In that sharing there will be, first of all, a tremendous transformation of all people concerned. There will also be an enrichment of our culture and our society. There will be a new possibility of making that available to all those around us.

Wallis: *South Africa is often described by journalists as one of the more hopeless situations in the world today. It has that reputation in the media. And yet you don't come across as a hopeless person, but as a person with a deeper theological kind of hope. What do you have to say to those of us in the middle of the same struggle, or in our own latest struggles, about hope and perseverance and how to sustain one's life in the midst of lengthy struggles?*

Naudé: Well, it is true that, on the face of it and for the foreseeable future, our situation in South Africa is bleak and certainly presents very little grounds for hope. I agree with that. But I think that is a superficial analysis; there's much more to it.

It is important that we constantly remind ourselves and others who believe that they are on the side of truth that we must not only maintain but also increase the demand for truth and seek to implement it in a spirit of love and understanding. The openness that you have toward other people, including your most bitter opponents, once you have discovered that truth, is a source of continuous strength and hope, because you know truth will eventually prevail. I think it is very important that we never forget that.

Second, if we believe that we are dealing with a God of justice and love, a God who wants to see the Kingdom become a glorious reality, then we know that whatever we are doing through God's grace is part of that process of renewal. It takes time. I may not be able to see it all happen, but I know with the strength of my faith and my convictions that moment will come.

Those of us who are suffering in South Africa are aware of the fact that the struggle may be a long one; but we know with a deep inner certainty that the day of liberation will come. Our people and our country will be free. We realize that sacrifice is needed. We realize many of us may not be able to see the eventual realization of freedom. But we know it will come.

Third, if you are involved in the struggle, you are constantly encouraged by the incredible commitment on the part of people, the quality of their leadership, the willingness to sacrifice time, energy, and life in order to attain that goal. That is a continuous source of inspiration.

I'm thinking, for instance, of young people who have been detained. How do they feel when they come out of jail? Are they willing to continue? With an immediacy and a deep sense of conviction, they say, "The period of detention, even the torture, has strengthened us. It has made it possible for us to move out with a greater commitment in order to obtain what we believe is the goal of a just society and a free South Africa."

Therefore, if you ask me whether there is hope for South Africa, I say, without any doubt. Tremendous potential exists in our country, but not only by way of the material riches that we can share; there is also tremendous potential for re-creating and transforming this evil, immoral, and totally objectionable system of apartheid and building something new: a society where there is the possibility of all of us—people of all colors, all religions, all classes—being able to live and work together. And to do so on the basis of our past experiences—our sufferings, the injustices of the past—to see that through God's grace they will not again occur.

Wallis: *Do you have advice, encouragement, or practical suggestions that have been helpful to you over the years to offer to those engaged in the struggle?*

Naudé: I would say, first of all, ensure that your understanding of faith, of the gospel, of the message of Christ's liberation is clear, relevant, and comprehensive of the whole of humankind. That's number one. Make your Christian faith real, meaningful, vibrant, and relevant.

The second piece of advice is to realize that this can never be done in isolation. God wants us to be Christians and to be human beings in community. You can never be fully human unless you've discovered the humanity in other human beings. You become human through him or her. Therefore the building of the sense of community, of mutual responsibility, of the sharing of joys and sorrows, of the need to grow together, is a vitally essential element in our life.

Third, stretch out your hand and discover those communities, areas, and countries where there is suffering, injustice, or a system of oppression. Discover to what degree there are similar patterns of life and suffering being enacted and being experienced in your own country. Don't close your eyes to the injustices of your own country by trying to solve the injustices of another country. That's an evasion of Christian responsibility.

Instead, see in the light of that discovery what is needed at home. Then begin to share, in the deep and meaningful sense of the word, by going out to Christians and others saying, "We are one with you. We are one in the realization of our weakness. But we are also one in the realization of the tremendous potential for change that God has given to all of us. Let us build together so that we may truly make this world God's Kingdom."

10

A Portrait of Anguish and Hope: Faces of South Africa

Joyce Hollyday

"The Lord answer you in the day of trouble! The name of God protect you! . . . Some boast of chariots, and some of horses; but we boast of the name of the Lord our God. They will collapse and fall; but we shall rise and stand upright."

Allan Boesak, Jr., age nine, read slowly from Psalm 20 at the conclusion of the family dinner. The look on his face was intent as he proclaimed the promises of God in a difficult time.

The words that appeared in the lectionary reading that night were particularly poignant. Just the day before, Allan's father had publicly announced to a packed cathedral that the Botha regime had signed its own death warrant (see the sermon, pp. 23–31). Three nights before that, a large brick came flying through the Boesaks' living room window, sending shattered glass in all directions. A death threat over the phone followed.

Allan, Jr., and his twelve-year-old sister, Pulane, had decided to sleep on the floor of the large walk-in closet in their parents' bedroom for a few nights. A group of theology students had volunteered to keep watch through the night at the house, armed only with the thermos of coffee they were given every night at 10:30 when they knocked at the door to announce their presence.

117

The knocks on that door are many, as are the faces that pass through that house. Women come asking for simple chores to do, and children for bread. Friends and family members are always welcome, and parishioners drop by often to show their support as threats from the South African government escalate.

Those faces—and many others across this land of anguish and hope—are the most poignant images of South Africa. They are a multitude of shades. One might consider the variety a gift. But in South Africa, the color of a face is a stamp for the future, the overriding factor determining one's existence. And each face has a story.

She had fashioned for herself a big hairbow out of a discarded plastic bag. The bag swathed her head and came to a knot with two points spread out to form the makeshift bow. She was only four, too shy to pose for a picture at close range. She lives in a shack in Crossroads, where government control and destitution make it impossible for little girls to dream of silk or satin bows.

Her friends can be found all across South Africa. They piece together bits of paper and plastic and string to make kites. They create crude push toys out of fragments of wire stuck through tin cans. They fashion a childhood from the bits and pieces of life that are left to them.

In Crossroads they are fortunate to reach the age of four. Diarrhea, dehydration, and the severe malnutrition known as *kwashiorkor* claim the lives of many children in this squatter camp outside Cape Town. In desperate times, sand is mixed with cornmeal to make a meal stretch further.

At the medical clinic, intake forms for children read "Siblings: alive _____, dead _____." Beyond the camp is a vast graveyard. Graves the size of children are dug in ominous expectation.

Crossroads came into being when the children's mothers moved from the homelands, or bantustans—the barren areas designated by South Africa's regime for the nation's blacks—to be closer to Cape Town, where a few of their husbands had found jobs. The women formed the core of resistance when the government tried to force the families back to the homelands, and they eventually won the right to be a "permanent" squatter camp. But beyond the "Not Open to the General Public" sign that marks the entrance to Crossroads remains an isolated island of human misery, caught in the crossfire between a cruel government, a corrupt local administration, brutal right-wing vigilantes, and the militant hope of the squatter camp's youths.

On one edge of Crossroads are rows of primitive migrant hostels. It is illegal for wives with their children to live in these dark and decrepit shelters with their migrant-worker husbands. Many stay in the homelands and see their husbands and fathers only a few weeks out of every year.

But some wives choose to live here illegally rather than suffer separation, crowding in, three families to a small room. Police frequently come to check on people in the hostels. When you ask the women there how many people live in a room, they reply, "Three men."

On another edge of Crossroads is the KTC satellite camp. Entire portions of the camp, thought by the government to be a "communist stronghold" because of the strong influence of the United Democratic Front, were razed. For weeks the fires raged and the bulldozers ravaged and the children cried. Razor wire now encircles the area, and military blockades control the flow of people in and out.

Razor wire and rifles, petrol bombs and huge armored casspirs (personnel carriers), and the whips known as *sjamboks*—all are part of the landscape for the children of apartheid. Childhood ends almost before it begins in black South Africa.

The children raise fists in defiant determination as soon as they are old enough to understand the struggle, an understanding that comes early. By school age they are organizers and participants in school "stayaways," commemorating and protesting such events as the massacre of children in Sharpeville in 1960 and Soweto in 1976.

Their energy has threatened the ruling powers of South Africa, who have targeted them in massive numbers for detention and torture. But there is no quashing that energy, which erupts most powerfully when they join together in a celebratory, defiant mass stomping called *toi-toi,* singing the freedom songs as they sway together, sending energy like a bolt of electricity surging through any crowd.

They do it at a detainees' meeting in Soweto with riot police just beyond the door. They *toi-toi* at a sports festival in Cape Town, and *toi-toi* past the bishop as he confers a blessing on all the children at the close of a Soweto church service. They defy police blockades set up around the city and come *toi-toi*-ing into a crowd of three thousand at a Cape Town cathedral. The message on their exuberant faces is, "We're here. And things are going to change."

It's resurrection hope that's written on those faces. Ask a ten-year-old in Mamelodi, the black township hear Pretoria, if he'll see apartheid end in his lifetime. Without hesitation he'll say "yes," and then add thoughtfully, "but maybe toward the end of it."

Then put this question to him: "Do you think your children will grow up without apartheid?"

His answer is clear: "I will see to it."

A video camera is aimed at this house twenty-four hours a day, and conversations in the front rooms can be monitored by the police across the street and next door. Reverend Eddie Leeux began talking about his detention, interrupting the story at one point to get a shoebox full of small pieces of toilet paper upon which he had kept a diary during his fifty-five days in prison. He had smuggled the paper out in the sleeves of a jacket he sent home to his wife, Lizzie, sending word without any explanation that she was not under any circumstances to wash the jacket until he got home.

Eddie Leeux was detained on Father's Day, June 15, 1986. His children had just finished giving him his Father's Day present and Lizzie had walked toward the kitchen to start breakfast, when the men with guns appeared in the doorway. As his father was being taken away, Eddie's youngest son, Zebedee, threw himself on a heap of laundry and wept. One of the arresting officers had the audacity to complain that Eddie was keeping him from spending Father's Day with his family.

Eddie's crimes included preaching against apartheid and using his car to transport dead and wounded people out of Duncan Village when the township exploded in riots in 1985. Eddie remembers that the bells at his church rang as he passed by on his way to prison.

Lizzie was given no information about where her husband was taken, and her tireless efforts to find him took her to many dead ends. The security police did all they could to break Eddie emotionally and convince him that his family had forgotten him. He reached such despair that at one point he wrote in his journal, "I can still see the hand of God, but I am beyond his reach."

Lizzie finally discovered where Eddie was being kept, but she was denied visits to him. Each day she prayed and hoped for his release. "You can only have hope until five o'clock," she said. "After five they master-lock the jail and no one will be released." She added, "In this country, if you don't have a strong faith in God, you go right down."

Young Zebedee was a source of strength. "Papa said before he went away that you must never cry and let them know that they have hurt you," he told his mother. Every day after school he asked her, "How are you? Did you cry today?"

Before we left their home, Eddie quoted the bishop of Port Elizabeth: "This country is mortally wounded. It is bleeding to death. And no one is allowed to heal the wound." But some people keep trying.

The older women in bright purple garb were just ending their prayer meeting in this famous living room in the black township of King Williams Town as we walked in the open front door. They were members of the Anglican Mothers Prayer Union.

We had been asked by our host if we would like to visit the home of Steve Biko, the well-known anti-apartheid student leader and proponent of "black consciousness" who was brutally murdered in 1977 while in police custody. It was a rare privilege to be going to the home of this martyr for freedom whose courageous witness had deeply influenced us. It was even more of a privilege—and a complete surprise—when our host led us over to one of the women and said, "I'd like you to meet Mrs. Biko, Steve's mother."

Alice Biko is a gracious and faithful woman who warmly welcomed us and talked proudly about her beloved son. She related both the torment and hope that have been part of being the mother of Steve Biko.

Her house was frequently searched, and she lived every day, she said, with "the fear of a mother whose son could be shot at any time." One morning he left and never came back. She phoned everywhere, trying to find him.

She eventually received a call from the security police assuring her that her son was fine. Two weeks later they called to tell her he was dead. She said of the agony they forced her son to endure and the anguish with which she still must live, "I am a bit bitter, but I must forgive."

In one of her last conversations with her son, she told him how difficult it was to be always worried about him being arrested and put in jail, how she never slept at night until she knew he was home. She related that he had responded by reminding her that Jesus had come to redeem his people and set them free.

"Are you Jesus?" she asked impatiently.

Steve gently answered her, "No, I'm not. But I'm going to do the same job." After that, she said, she never asked him any more questions.

She related that she now understands so much more about what he was saying to her then. He had once said to her, in words not unlike Jesus' to Mary, "I am not your son only; I have many mothers. And you have many children." Steve Biko gave his life so that those many mothers and their children might not suffer.

Alice Biko finished her poignant reflections with thoughts about the week we were about to enter—Holy Week. "It seems as if during Lent," she said, "the suffering of Jesus becomes very acute. It is not unlike the suffering my own son went through."

As we were about to leave, Jim Wallis told her how deeply his life had been affected by her son and thanked her for giving Steve Biko to the world. She reached over, took his hand, and said, "You are my son, too."

Military eyes peer constantly from the tower that rises above the black township of Duncan Village. The eyes are aided at night by powerful floodlights that can search out "suspicious activity" in any corner. We arrived in early afternoon and, under the tower's watchful eye, were greeted by a young man active in the struggle.

We walked unhindered for almost an hour, with Tommy pointing out overcrowded homes and fetid latrines and encouraging us to take pictures to carry out of the country for the world to see. The South African Police, in one of their omnipresent yellow vehicles, were the first to stop and question us. Fifteen minutes later a casspir appeared on the horizon and made its way toward us. Eight members of the South African Defense Forces, wearing khaki fatigues and pointing rifles, jumped out and surrounded us, ordering us to the military "strong point."

We were escorted at gunpoint in the direction of the tower, taken past the rows of barbed wire that surround the military headquarters, and ushered into an interrogation room. A soldier told us we were being detained, pending arrival of a member of the "special branch," the term applied to South Africa's security police.

I kept my eyes on Tommy. Though his demeanor became immediately subdued, a glint of courageous pride remained in his eyes.

The security police officer spoke rapidly in Afrikaans to the other police and army personnel. He asked us brusquely if we didn't know it was illegal under the current state of emergency to take pictures in a black area. We had been informed only that it was illegal to take pictures of police or military activity — and told by several people in the struggle that keeping up with this government's constantly changing body of regulations would be a full-time job.

He mentioned how much foreigners like to come to the townships and then take "unnecessary propaganda" about his country overseas. He accused us of "creating a rumble among the people" and added, "for all we know, you might be ANC" — a reference to the banned African National Congress, perceived by the South African government as apartheid's worst enemy.

After his interrogation of us, he turned to Tommy, shaking his finger and ejecting stern and threatening warnings. "Didn't you just get out?" he said, referring to Tommy's recent release from ten months in detention. He finished with a promise that Tommy would be back in detention before long if he didn't give up his subversive activities.

Tommy's only response was to reach calmly into his back pocket, remove his pocket New Testament, and, putting it in front of the officer's face, say simply, "I am a Christian." A brief moment of silence descended as the arrogance of evil met the quiet power of the gospel.

We were given a police escort out of Duncan Village. We took Tommy out with us, making sure he had a place to hide for a few months from the security police.

"Why did you do it?" Jim asked him on the way out. "Why would you take the risk of taking around a couple of white Americans you never even met before?"

Tommy talked about nonracialism at the core of the new South Africa he and his friends are building, about how important it is that people in the townships see whites who are with them in the struggle. "We are not fighting against whites; we are fighting against injustice," he said. He offered his observation that the police and even State President P. W. Botha are workers oppressed by the system.

He spoke of his detention, when he and many of his friends were rounded up, kept in cold cells, fed cornmeal infested with worms, and denied access to a doctor. Like many others we met, he was reluctant to talk about his torture.

"Our solidarity grew there," he said. As in every other jail in South Africa, the police strategy to thwart resistance was turned on its head. After participating in hunger strikes and hours of political discussion, young people came out more politicized and determined than ever to rid their country of apartheid.

"We are just going forward," said Tommy with determination written on his face. "It's not the time to be afraid."

The Transkei's rolling green hills, dotted with thatched-roof *rondavels,* are deceptively beautiful. The land in this independent homeland is barren, good only for grazing herds. In the northern homelands, the barrenness is more stark—long stretches of sandy, dusty land lacking vegetation, shacks and huts built hastily on soft earth.

Many of the men are absent, in the cities looking for jobs that don't exist in the homelands. Women and children are most visible, carrying bundles of wood on their heads, herding sheep, sitting by the side of the road offering pineapples with hollow reeds stuck into their juicy cores for sale.

The people are poor, the homeland governments without resources, and corruption common. Electricity and running water are rarities. "Independence" means only being cut off from South Africa's resources, and it has no meaning when the South African security police decide to cross borders. Most blacks have rejected independence on these terms, refusing to live in the homelands despite government pressure to do so.

Leaving the Transkei, we made our way north to the town of Lady Grey. We drove under a canopy of low-hanging trees as we approached the stream at the entrance to the tiny village. Playing children parted and waved as we drove through, sending a spray of water in all directions.

The members of a poor church in this isolated rural area are struggling to survive. A four-acre plot of land that lies not far from their church is overgrown with weeds. They have a dream to grow vegetables there to feed their families.

While we were visiting Lady Grey, the new pastor of the church was miles away in Port Elizabeth, trying to get government permission to acquire the land and transform the weed plot into a community garden. Though no whites were anywhere in the area, word came back that the weed plot was in an area designated white; no blacks could own it.

The children smiled and waved again as we left Lady Grey. And I sent up a prayer for children who live under a government that will not surrender four acres of weeds—"white" weeds—so that they might eat.

Every afternoon at 3:30 the truck comes to the dump near the Buffalo Flats area of East London. About a thousand kids—orphans and run-aways, blacks and Indians and so-called coloreds—live in the bush surrounding the dump. The oldest are teenagers, the youngest their infant sons and daughters—children of children.

Sustenance comes just after 3:30, when the children scavenge through the day's garbage. Nutrition is scarce, and chemicals and gasoline often get dumped over the "edible" stuff, slowly eating away at the young stomachs that swallow the tainted garbage.

An older kid came one day to Reggie Naidoo—a young Indian seminarian with dark, intense eyes—asking for food. He took a carload of bread to the dump; the kids, eyes as vacant as their stomachs, surrounded his car and rocked it wildly. Naidoo has been taking food there ever since.

Reggie Naidoo wants to build a "Child Safety Home" that will house 250 kids—as a start. He has offers of free mattresses and donated labor from architects and plumbers. But his dream goes unrealized. He won't build a home in a particular racial area that will exclude others; government officials refuse to allow a nonracial children's home.

They don't seem to be bothered about a nonracial dump.

The huge tenements make up one of the most densely populated areas in South Africa. Women have to get up before dawn to secure space on a washline. Forty-five thousand families are on a waiting list for the small flats in the broad, three-story brick buildings. Meanwhile, homes in white areas stand empty.

Unemployment is above 65 percent and rising every year in Lavendar Hill. Gangs with names like the Mafia, the Mongrels, and the Young Americans—borrowed from American TV—have taken control of the streets, with the largest gang boasting eight hundred members.

The tenements of Lavendar Hill all bear names of streets from District Six. The residents used to live in District Six, a thriving, multiracial neighborhood of Cape Town that was destroyed when the Group Areas Act was enacted and the area was declared white.

Just beyond Lavendar Hill is a place called Vrygrond, meaning "free ground"—ironic, since residents have to pay rent for space to construct a miserable, little shack. The shacks can be no larger than four meters by four meters here—government regulation.

Miriam came out of her shack when she saw us coming. She had just gotten word that sixty families in an adjacent area were going to be pushed out that night, their homes bulldozed. In a gesture of generosity beyond her means, she had offered to take three women and their children into her already overcrowded, tiny corrugated-iron shack. The rest would have to build shacks behind the sand dunes and tear them down by morning before the police saw them.

Bulldozing squatter areas is one of the government's strategies for making life in South Africa so intolerable for blacks that they will move to the homelands. New legislation introduced while we were in the country would fine illegal squatters up to ten thousand rand (about $5,000) or sentence them to five years in prison.

Unemployment in Vrygrond is 90 percent. "Most people don't even know if they'll have a piece of bread tonight," said Miriam. She and others in Vrygrond used to have monthly meetings with people from other squatter camps to try to organize for change, but the government banned the meetings.

"If only Botha could come and walk here. . . ." Her voice trailed off, leaving her thought unfinished. She didn't want to accept that Botha and his friends were plotting her suffering. Her spirit of generosity made her incapable of believing that anyone would have an approach to life different from hers.

"This is our South Africa, too," she said. "That is the sadness—God created it for all of us."

Miriam knew it was only a matter of time before the police would come and raze her home again. She had been pushed out from numerous places. "The government never tells us where we can go," she said. "But this time we are not moving. This is our dead end. They can put us all in jail if they want to. And they will—the children too."

A woman with nothing was having even that taken away from her. "I see a very dark future—very, very dark," she said. "It's not only me—I think the majority of us see it that way."

Vrygrond, like all black areas, lies out of view of white society. On the other side of the main road, a two-minute drive, is Marina de Gama. Sprawling homes painted dazzling white, draped with bougainvillea and roses, cluster around a human-made lake, with moorings for sailboats outside every door. There are no restrictions here on the size of homes.

We asked Miriam before we left her if she had any hope for her children. The despair was evident in her eyes as she said, "No . . . No, I have no hope."

She sat on the edge of the pew, a simple white bow fixed between the tight cornrows that covered her head. Her small legs, crossed at the ankles, occasionally swung gently; her unseeing eyes wandered in all directions.

Her fingers kept returning to the red rose pinned to her plain, blue dress. She stroked the soft petals, occasionally pulling one off and putting it to her face, smiling as she breathed its sweet fragrance.

She and her friends, each wearing a blue uniform, were from a school for the blind that lies outside Cape Town. They were the featured choir for the Good Friday service at the church where Allan Boesak is pastor. At the appropriate moment, teachers from the school brusquely grabbed the arms of the children and herded them to the front of the church, where they sang a few songs and then returned to their seats. Her fingers returned to her rose.

When she prayed, her head bowed and her tiny hands came together in perfect form, fingers extended, just as she had been taught. By the time the preacher from America got up to speak, her head began to nod with weariness.

I wondered if it would be frightening to her to be gathered up and held by a stranger she couldn't see. Her only response to my action was to sigh and fall asleep quickly in my arms.

Jim Wallis focused his sermon on Jesus' cry from the cross, "My God, my God, why have you forsaken me?" He reminded the congregation that, despite God's faithfulness to the very end, the gut-wrenching cry of God's son was real, the feeling overpowering. I heard it echo in my soul for the sake of this land.

Jim held forth a resounding promise: "If the South African government puts the church of Jesus Christ on the cross, it will be overthrown by the resurrection!" The words had the powerful ring of theological truth, and a rush of affirmation surged through the congregation. But I could not see it. All I could see for this land was an unending Good Friday; I did not yet have eyes to see the resurrection. I wondered if the child in my arms ever would.

I led her back to her seat for the closing hymn. Now she had only to wait for someone to grab her arm and take her home. She sat quietly with her head down, her small legs swinging, a stem without petals pinned to her plain, blue dress.

She could not see an older, more confident schoolmate rush to the front of the church. With some assistance, the teenager groped her way toward Allan Boesak, whom she had dreamed of meeting some day.

She asked to touch his face. She gently ran her fingers over every feature and then touched his hair. As joyful pride spread over her face, she said, "It's true; you're not white."

"What made you think I'm white?" Boesak asked.

"I thought anyone who's so famous must be white."

She wanted to meet "the preacher" as well. She was led to Jim. She touched his face and hair, commenting with quiet surprise, "I never heard a white man talk that way."

In South Africa, even the blind are not allowed to be color blind.

Two million people live here. Rows of identical, box-like houses, the homes of Soweto, stretch as far as one can see — and beyond. One home is under constant police surveillance, but its door is always open for friends and for Soweto's children fleeing the police. Next door is a school, and many children have jumped the fence during police raids and found refuge in the home of Albertina Sisulu.

"When the government started being brutal to the children in 1976," said Sisulu — referring to the police response to the children's protest of inferior education during "the Soweto uprising" — "children were just doomed like flies in the streets. Whatever street you turned on, you saw the corpses of children shot by the police, by the people who are supposed to be the protectors.

"If your child is missing," she continued, "you must get to one of the police cells, where you find a pile of corpses of children in [school] uniform. You must go through to see if your child is there underneath. And in most cases, you find your child under some other corpse."

Albertina Sisulu is a nurse and midwife; she has seen far too many children die from police brutality and infants from malnutrition. She has ushered countless new lives into the world, each survivor likely, in time, to join the struggle for freedom. She has raised five children of her own and three whom she adopted after the deaths of relatives.

But Albertina Sisulu has also been midwife and mother to a movement, with an impact that spans generations. Three decades ago she was a leader in the famous march against the extension of "passes" to women. The passes, instituted to control the black population and restrict its movement, were an early symbol of the evil of apartheid. The government made a mistake when it tried to force women to carry them.

Organized by the just-formed Federation of South African Women, twenty thousand women marched to the government's Union Building in Pretoria in August 1956. "But the prime minister ran away from us," said Sisulu with a smile. "I think when he saw the women, he just decided to run away."

At that march the women sang a defiant chant that has become a cornerstone of the women's movement in South Africa: "You have struck the women; you have struck the rock!" "You can imagine," said Sisulu, "twenty thousand voices rocking through the Union Building!"

That protest was just the beginning for Sisulu. She has been harassed, tried for treason, imprisoned, placed under house arrest for ten years, and banned for seventeen—the longest banning order ever handed out in South Africa. Her husband, Walter Sisulu, was sentenced to life imprisonment in 1964 in the same trial that put African National Congress leader Nelson Mandela behind bars. Two of her sons are in jail, and three other children in exile.

She has been granted the high honor of being named one of the three presidents of the United Democratic Front. And she was given an "honor" by the other side as well: so threatening is her strength to the defenders of apartheid, the South African government singled her out and gave her individual restrictions when it banned the seventeen anti-apartheid organizations in late February 1988.

When you ask her what helps her bear the tremendous burden of decades of suffering, she smiles warmly. "I wouldn't be alive if I weren't staying with God," she says. "He's a wonderful man. He's the only man who takes care of me."

She then speaks about the defenders of apartheid. "They call themselves Christians, but I fail to understand, because in the very Bible they are carrying it says, 'Thou shalt not kill.' But they are busy killing the children, busy killing the people in jail."

She continues, "In the Bible there is no black and white. God calls us his children—all of us." Those keeping watch on Albertina Sisulu's door will never understand what greatness is inside.

The woman spoke with fire in her eyes, cutting through the air with waves of her hand, calling other mothers to unite against the detention of their children. The setting was Soweto, the time just weeks after the Detainees' Parents Support Committee had been effectively banned. Rallies are illegal, but this "tea party" went on nonetheless, with social workers stepping in to organize in the DPSC's place.

She spoke in Xhosa, the gentle clicks of the tribal language rolling rhythmically off her tongue. Interjected throughout were words uttered in English. Words like "banning," "detention," "state of emergency," "violence," and "unemployment." I began to keep a list.

I showed the list to our interpreter as we left Soweto. "Yes," he explained, "we have no root in our language for words such as these."

We knew his face only from pictures. A candle he gave his mother last Christmas was lit at every meal as a reminder while he remained in prison. A scrapbook she put together for him tells the story of his arrests; it includes news clippings, letters of support, and the tiny deck of playing cards he made out of toilet paper during his first detention.

Martin Wittenberg is a trusted, white leader of the United Democratic Front in conflict-ridden Pietermaritzburg. The detention of Martin and other UDF leaders had delivered a serious blow to peace negotiations in an area that had seen 397 people killed in the previous four months.

Before Easter, Martin's mother, Monica Wittenberg, mentioned to the authorities holding her son that it is a tradition at Easter to release a prisoner. Denied her petition, she asked that they at least allow his sister Reinhild to visit. The police refused that request as well, stating that it would be "too traumatic" for a teenager to see her brother in prison — this from a spokesperson for a system that is notorious for its torture of children.

We stayed in Martin's room during our time in Pietermaritzburg. I wished for the opportunity to meet him. It was abundantly clear that his witness has had a strong impact on his family and many others, as has his tenacious sense of humor in the most tragic of times.

Hanging on the front of his file cabinet, next to his UDF stickers and slogans, is a work of an African poet. It begins, "In order to ensure absolute national security, the government has passed the Animal and Insect Emergency Control and Discipline Act. . . ."

It outlines the new regulations: buffaloes, cows, and goats are henceforth prohibited from grazing in herds of more than three; birds can no longer flock, nor bees swarm, for such constitutes unlawful assembly; penguins and zebras are ordered to discard their non-regulation uniforms; and under no circumstances are elephants to break wind between the hours of 6 p.m. and 6 a.m., "for such could easily be interpreted as gunshot and might spark off a riot."

Walking up the steep hill is like taking a pilgrimage to a shrine. And indeed there once was a sort of shrine here. Now it is only a concrete foundation with the remains of a chimney rising from one corner.

This area outside Durban is the sight of Gandhi's first ashram, a farm and community and training center, among whose later pupils was Steve Biko. Until 1985 Gandhi's wood-and-iron home stood on this spot. Inside were his spinning wheels, books, and the brass nameplate from his law office in town. The house was called Sarvodaya, meaning "welfare of all," a poetic reminder of how this nonracial settlement stood for decades in contrast to the rest of society.

In 1985, however, the peaceful nonracialism of the Phoenix Settlement evaporated in a tide of racial violence that engulfed the area. Fires were set and homes were looted. Sarvodaya was destroyed.

But four years later, out of the ashes the phoenix is rising again. The site of Gandhi's first printing press has been turned into a community-run school, and the sounds of children singing and chanting spill over the hill. His home was dismantled, not burned; one observer says pieces of Sarvodaya and its spirit now form parts of probably a hundred homes. And in the clinic named after him, a bust of the humble, little man — round glasses perched on the end of his nose — sits awkwardly on a folding metal chair, keeping watch over the babies as they line up in their mothers' arms to get weighed.

Black South Africans are exiles in the land of their birth. And black South African women are exiles among the exiles. Raised in a culture that forces their dependence on men, oppressed by a government that wrenches that dependence from them, they are often compelled to survive by their own strength and resources.

With children on their backs, they work the fields and weave bright tapestries. In the homelands they herd sheep and raise sparse crops. They wander from home to home in the suburbs, looking for light housework that earns some enough money to feed their children.

Too many must watch helplessly as their children die of malnutrition. And far too many are forced to wander from police station to prison in search of husbands and children snatched from them in the night.

But more and more, women are claiming their strength and joining a movement begun by their sisters generations ago. The weekend of April 16, 1988, on the anniversary of the establishment of the Federation of South African Women (FEDSAW), a massive women's cultural festival took place in Cape Town. Preparations for the festival had gone on for weeks, with meeting locations kept secret to avoid government interference in the wake of the February bannings.

Throughout the festival, crafts and books were on display, generous portions of spicy food were ladled out to patrons, and traditional music and dance reverberated through the hall. The aims of the festival, according to the organizers, were to help South African women, faced with so much brutality, to celebrate their creativity and unity, and to develop "a common perspective which is so necessary in order to develop a national culture out of the ashes of apartheid."

The huge event was opened by Helen Joseph, who more than three decades before was elected the first secretary of FED-SAW. People parted to make way as this white-haired stalwart of the struggle was brought in her wheelchair to the stage. With her fist raised and a radiant smile on her face, she brought the gathering to its feet in a resounding ovation. Helen Joseph was a social worker in South Africa's Cape region in the 1950s. Through a decade of compassion, she began to realize that she was, in her own words, "just giving aspirin for a toothache." The wretched conditions she saw and her intimate concern for the people she served finally would not let her settle for anything less than giving her life to the freedom struggle.

Joseph eventually moved to Johannesburg. "I put my political boots on," she says. "And I've never taken them off since."

Helen Joseph is known in South Africa as the "Mother of the Struggle." In a nation that reveres its mothers and draws its strength from the struggle, the title is perhaps the highest accolade. And it has been conferred on a woman who came as a stranger to the black community, who opened herself to be transformed by its strength and hope.

The South African government has also noted Helen Joseph's strength of commitment. In 1962 she became the first person to be put under house arrest in South Africa. That restriction lasted ten years.

Joseph digs back into a rich treasure trove of memories when you ask her to tell her favorite stories from the struggle. Like Albertina Sisulu, she was a leader in the 1956 march against the extension of passes. "We went, we saw, and we conquered!" she says of that day with a triumphant smile.

Then, like a young school girl with a secret, she bends over and explains in a hush about the second verse of the song, which was directed to the prime minister and made famous there: "It goes, 'Strydom, you have struck a rock; you have tampered with the women; you shall die!' " With an ironic grin and not a touch of malice, she adds, "And a year later he was dead!"

Joseph remembers an event just before the march, when she was a speaker for the Congress of the People. "That stands out," she says. "I was on the platform when the police came. I made the rest of my speech with policemen at four corners, standing with guns pointed at me."

She recalls the launching of the United Democratic Front in 1983: "It was so magnificent. We had fifteen thousand people. And that was when I was given the title 'Mother of the Struggle.' " She moves on to an equally memorable event: "The other peak for me, really, was last week. A friend organized a surprise party for me. I had a hundred guests!"

Joseph had just turned eighty-three, and she was thankful to celebrate another birthday after a long and serious illness. At eighty-three, what keeps this magnificent woman going? "The struggle!" she says without hesitation. "The struggle and the love of my friends."

"And what do you think women in particular have to contribute to the struggle?" I ask her. "Everything!" she says with a broad smile and a characteristic twinkle in her eye. "Their lives, their courage, their discipline, their gifts, their determination.

"The feeling of joy in the midst of the struggle is tremendous," she continues. "No breast-beating, no brow-beating, no self-pity. Just determination and defiance. It's beautiful. It can't lose. I'm telling you, it cannot lose. In the end, it will win. The spirit of women cannot be crushed. That's what I have learned over the years. I will stay in the struggle until the day I die; but I hope we get freedom first."

"Do you think we will?" I ask.

"We've got to," she laughs. "I don't propose to live until I'm ninety-five!"

Dusk brings a change of mood to the township. Domestics and laborers, weary from a day's work in the city, make their way home in the last moments of daylight. A stream of women, water jugs balanced on their heads, some with babies on their backs, moves slowly out from the central spigot over the township's rutted roads in the encroaching cool of the evening. Children leave their play and move inside, and dogs seem to take the sun's disappearance as a signal to commence barking.

In the waning light, the box-like houses take on even more sameness. The large, crude, hand-painted numbers distinguishing them — the work of the police, who got tired of mothers rubbing out less visible numbers to protect their children from police searches — are legible now only by the light of police searchlights.

At the entrance to the township, spread out on a table, are rows of sheep's heads, blood still running from their necks and the look of terror from the slaughter still on their faces. Women tending fires cut pieces of meat from the carcasses and skewer them for sale.

A family that cannot afford the mutton buys scores of the sheep's legs. Scraping the hair from the legs, they cook the pile of bones with scant meat over a fire for their evening meal.

At dusk the air gets heavy with smoke and a pungent, burning odor as paraffin lamps are lit, one by one, up and down the rows of tiny houses. The smell of fire seems to permeate black South Africa. I think of the homeless people we saw in downtown Johannesburg gathered around a fire in a barrel, and the children in the bush surrounding East London taking turns stoking a small blaze for warmth. I remember those children's bellies, swollen from hunger, and the dazed look on the faces of their parents, who had been routed by the police from their dilapidated, makeshift homes in the middle of the night and had returned to find nothing but smoldering ashes.

As we were on the verge of leaving South Africa, the faces of people frequently flashed through my mind — Miriam and Tommy and Eddie and the little blind girl. I wrestled often with despair, struggling to find the internal resources to keep the evil that was so pervasive in this country at bay. The thought of how many people were going to lose their lives before this country changed — some of them, perhaps, friends we had come to love — often brought a convulsion of tears.

But there was one constant for me, one pervasive ring of hope. That was the singing of *"Nkosi Sikelel' i Afrika"* — "God Bless Africa," the African national anthem. Old people sang it at the end of Soweto church services and young athletes sang it before a sports celebration; children belted it out at the detainees' meeting and women sang it with pride at the beginning of their first national festival in Cape Town. It is always sung with dignity and strength, and chills run up and down the spine at the swelling affirmation that this is God's land, to be shared by all.

The young comrade taking us through the township at dusk is speaking of the struggle, of the land and freedom that have been stolen from his people. As he speaks, I am reminded of the glimpses of this land's beauty that we have been privileged to behold — its vast expanses of beaches, pounding surf, plains populated with ostrich herds and mountains poking through clouds. A sliver of a crescent moon resting one night on the edge of Cape Town's famous Table Mountain urged a stream of tears from me, so tragic is it that some South Africans have robbed the glory of this land from others. What a strong nation this would be if all its wealth and beauty were shared.

As we walk toward our friend's home, the sky turns blood-red. We stop, speechless, in awe of the red expanse that forms a brilliant canopy over South Africa. After a moment, he says, "But they cannot take the sky from us."

It is the only claim that black South Africans still have on their home, where they cannot vote, or own land, or even be sure of a four-by-four-meter shack to live in.

This is an absurdly tragic nation — where tallies of recent flood victims included only the white ones; and where, at a famous natural wonder, an extra hole was blasted into the cave's wall so that blacks would have a separate entrance. It is a land in which it is illegal for some husbands and wives to live together, and where, for the sake of "public safety," people are shot in the streets. A land that has the audacity to ban human beings and attach racial labels to pieces of earth, to tear-gas church congregations and torture children, to declare candles lit in solidarity and hope a threat to the state.

"Ten years of Botha, forty years of apartheid, and a lifetime of suffering," sadly proclaims a popular poster. And, according to many, the suffering has just begun.

But that acknowledgment comes laden, not with despair, but with overwhelming hope. It comes from the assurance that this triumph was already won many years ago on a cross.

South Africans hungering for freedom are willing to follow the one who won it—even to their own deaths. And from that suffering comes a promise: a new day is going to dawn in this land of anguish and hope.

Appendix

Letters between Church Leaders and the State President

An unprecedented era in church-state conflict in South Africa was initiated with the February 29, 1988, March to Parliament by church leaders and clergy. The march launched a battle carried out not only in the streets but also in a flurry of letters exchanged between State President P. W. Botha and the church leaders.

The atmosphere took on the feel of a holy war as Botha appeared almost nightly on South African television in the weeks following the march. Claiming that he, too, is a faithful follower of Christ, Botha lambasted the church leaders, accusing them of betraying the gospel and espousing communist ideology. No air time was given to the other side of this controversy that rocked the nation.

The theological claims put forward in the letters provide a remarkable picture of not only a church-state conflict but also a church-church controversy. The editors of this book carried the letters out of South Africa and reprint them in the following pages.

PETITION FROM CHURCH LEADERS TO THE STATE PRESIDENT AND MEMBERS OF PARLIAMENT

February 29, 1988

Khotso House
De Villiers Street
Johannesburg

The State President and Members of Parliament
Parliament Street
Cape Town

Dear Mr. State President and Members of Parliament:

We, as leaders of a number of South African churches, have come to Parliament today to witness and pray in a time of crisis outside the buildings in which you make important decisions affecting the lives of millions of South Africans who belong to our churches. In terms of the principles of nonviolent direct action, we informed the Government of our intentions before coming here. Once we have completed our act of worship outside where you work, we intend returning to St. George's Cathedral.

We are deeply distressed at, and protest to you in the strongest of terms at, the restrictions which were placed last week on the activities of seventeen of our people's organisations, on the Congress of South African Trade Unions, and on eighteen of our leaders.

We believe that the Government, in its actions over recent years but especially by last week's action, has chosen a path for the future which will lead to violence, bloodshed, and instability. By imposing such drastic restrictions on organisations which have campaigned peacefully for the end of apartheid, you have removed nearly all effective means open to our people to work for true change by nonviolent means. Only yesterday one of our number pleaded publicly with our people not to react to your measures by resorting to violence, but if some of our people turn to violence you must take the responsibility.

We are particularly horrified at the restrictions you have placed on people and organisations who have been in the forefront of the struggle to bring peace to the strife-torn areas of Pietermaritzburg and KTC in Cape Town. Mr. Archie Gumede, Mr. Willie Hofmeyr, and Mrs. Albertina Sisulu are just a few of many people who are now banned from working for peace. Your actions indicate to us that those of you in government have decided that only violence will keep you in power; that you have chosen the "military option" for our country.

It appears to us that you are encouraging the growth of black surrogate forces to split the black community and to smash effective opposition to apartheid, moreover that you are trying to ensure as far as possible that it is the blood of black people, and not of white people, that is spilled in your struggle to hold onto power.

We regard restrictions not only as an attack on democratic activity in South Africa but as a blow directed at the heart of the Church's mission in South Africa. The activities which have been prohibited are central to the proclamation of the Gospel in our country and we must make it clear that, no matter what the consequences, we will explore every possible avenue for continuing the activities which you have prohibited other bodies from undertaking. We will not be stopped from campaigning for the release of prisoners, from calling for clemency for those under sentence of death, from calling for the unbanning of political organisations, from calling for the release of political leaders to negotiate the transfer of power to all the people of our country, from commemorating significant events in the life of our nation, from commemorating those who have died in what you call "riots," or from calling on the international community to apply pressure to force you to the negotiating table.

Last week many of us issued a statement in which we addressed primarily the oppressed people of our land, for we believe it is they who will decide in the final analysis when apartheid is going to be abolished. We urged them to intensify the struggle for justice and peace and we encouraged them not to lose hope, for victory against evil in this world is guaranteed by our Lord.

Our message applies also to you. Your position is becoming untenable. Your fellow South Africans want nothing more than to live in a just and peaceful country and we urge you—without too much hope of being heard—to turn from the path you have chosen. If those of you in government persist with your current policies, then we urge those of you out of government to withdraw from white politics and to join the real struggle for democracy.

We urge you to take the following immediate action:

• Lift last week's restrictions and end the State of Emergency.

• Unban political organisations, release and remove restrictions on our political leaders, allow exiles to return, and free all detainees.

• Enter negotiations for a dispensation in which all of us can live together in peace, freedom, and justice.

We have not undertaken this action lightly. We have no desire to be martyrs. However, the Gospel leaves us no choice but to seek ways of witnessing effectively and clearly to the values of our Lord and Saviour Jesus Christ, and you give us virtually no other effective and peaceful means of doing so.

God bless you.

Archbishop T. W. Ntongana—Apostolic Methodist Church of South Africa

Archbishop N. H. Ngada—United Independent Believers in Christ

The Rev. Ron L. Steel—chairman, United Congregational Church of Southern Africa

The Rev. James Gribble—chairman, Good Hope District, Methodist Church of Southern Africa

The Rev. Peter Storey—past president, SACC and Methodist Church

Bishop Lawrence Henry—Catholic Church, Cape Town

Pastor M. D. Assur—general secretary, Evangelical Lutheran Church in Southern Africa

Bishop Olaf Theo Xulu—president, Council of African Independent Churches (CAIC)

Pastor T. M. Chere—Northern Transvaal Council of Churches

Bishop Charles Albertyn—Anglican Church, Cape Town

Bishop George Swartz—dean of the Anglican Province of Southern Africa and bishop of Kimberley and Kuruman

The Rev. Frank Chikane—general secretary, SACC

Dr. Allan Boesak—moderator of the Ned Geref Sendingkerk [Dutch Reformed Mission Church]

Bishop H. B. Senatle—African Methodist Episcopal Church

The Rev. Dr. Khoza Mgojo—president, Methodist Church of Southern Africa (MCSA)

The Rev. John P. Scholtz—past president, MCSA

Moulana Faried Essack—Muslim Judicial Council, Call of Islam

The Rev. Canon Geoff Quinlan—suffragan bishop-elect, Cape Town (Anglican)

The Ven. Edward MacKenzie—suffragan bishop-elect, Cape Town

The Rev. Samson A. Khumalo—general secretary, Presbyterian Church of Africa

Archbishop Desmond Tutu—metropolitan, Anglican Church

The Rev. Paul Makhubu—general secretary, CAIC

The Very Rev. Edward King—Anglican dean of Cape Town

The Rev. Mmutlanyane Stanley Mogaba—general secretary, MCSA

Archbishop Stephen Naidoo—Catholic archbishop of Cape Town

LETTER FROM P. W. BOTHA TO DESMOND TUTU

16 March 1988

Tuynhuys
Cape Town

PERSONAL

Archbishop Desmond Tutu
Anglican Archbishop of Cape Town
Bishopscourt
Claremont
7700

Dear Archbishop Tutu:

I hereby wish to acknowledge receipt of your letter of 1 March 1988 with the attached petition dated 29 February 1988.

Before I comment on your petition, I wish to ask whether it is your considered opinion that the so-called March on Parliament was really necessary, and worthy of the cause and message of Christ and the churches represented by those who were involved, knowing that the actions were illegal?

You know that you, and others who were with you on that day, have on more than one occasion been well received at Tuynhuys and the Union Buildings — sometimes in a blaze of publicity but sometimes also unknown to others in order to maintain a measure of confidentiality that is apparently necessary at times to protect some of those who have discussions with the Government. The truth of the assertion in your petition that you have "virtually no other effective and peaceful means" of "witnessing effectively," therefore stands under serious doubt.

Furthermore, in your petition you referred to trade unions; and you are no doubt aware of the fact that only last week I extended an invitation to various important trade unions in our country, to have talks with me and members of the Government in Tuynhuys. Some of the very people you referred to were among those who did not turn up for the meeting, some even without having the courtesy of replying to the invitation.

I am sure you will agree that the whole basis of your action is therefore seriously in question, and that it was to a large degree planned as a calculated public relations exercise.

But it goes much further than that, as you know so well. To illustrate the point, I wish to quote from a recent broadcast by the ANC's propaganda radio, Radio Freedom: "The church must now be developed into a fierce battleground against the regime. . . . We must organise our forces for a physical confrontation with the forces of the apartheid regime."

The question inevitably arises whether it is possible to come to any other conclusion than that actions such as the March to Parliament may be seen as part of the campaign referred to in the ANC propaganda broadcast? But there is also a wider element involved, as illustrated by *Sechaba* of September 1985, where it stated that: "Members of the ANC fully understand why both the ANC and SACP [South African Communist Party] are two hands in the same body, why they are two pillars of our revolution."

You are no doubt aware that the expressed intention of the planned revolution by the ANC/SACP alliance is to ultimately transform South Africa into an atheistic Marxist state, where freedom of faith and worship will surely be among the first casualties.

If you disagree with this, you should state so clearly and publicly, because it also directly relates to your petition, and in particular the statement that: "victory against *evil* in this world is guaranteed by our Lord."

What is clearly at issue here is your understanding of *evil*: is atheistic Marxism the evil, or does your view of evil include the struggle on behalf of Christianity, the Christian faith, and freedom of faith and worship, against the forces of godlessness and Marxism?

In the petition you used phrases such as the following: "*people's* organisations," "*democratic* activity," the "*struggle* for *justice* and *peace*," and "the *real struggle* for *democracy*."

In this regard I wish to quote again from the already mentioned broadcast of Radio Freedom: "In the name of *justice* we must take up the *fight*: we must participate in such means of *struggle*; the *democratic* movement must be given a voice in all churches; church services must be services that further the *democratic* call; the *church* must be for *liberation*."

You owe all Christians an explanation of your exact standpoint, for we are all adults, and the time for bluffing and games is long past. The question must be posed whether you are acting on behalf of the kingdom of God, or the kingdom promised by the ANC and the SACP? If it is the latter, say so, but do not then hide behind the structures and the cloth of the Christian church, because Christianity and Marxism are irreconcilable opposites.

In your petition you urged the Government to take a number of immediate steps. In reply to that, I urge those who support this petition to reply to the following questions:

• Does the phrase "the transfer of power to all the people of our country" as used in your petition have the same meaning as the same phrase used by the ANC and the SACP, that is for the ultimate creation of a Marxist regime in South Africa?

• Are you and those who co-signed the petition in favour of the establishment of a Marxist dictatorship in South Africa under the rule of the ANC and the SACP, and to the detriment of the church?

• Do you believe it to be in line with your interpretation of the churches "prophetic mission" and so-called "liberation theology" to which you subscribe, to further the cause of the ANC and the SACP, and thus Marxism and atheism?

In conclusion I wish to ask you whether it is not true that the Christian church knows no other power than love and faith, and no other message than the true message of Christ; and if it brings its spiritual power into the secular power-play, and the message of Christ into disrepute, then it becomes a secular instead of a sacred spiritual subject, thereby relinquishing its claim to be church?

If you accept this statement as true, you should establish whether you were acting in the name of God and the church, or whether it was in your individual capacities as members of society embracing secularism, thereby doing a disservice to the very churches which you claim to have represented.

Yours sincerely,

P. W. Botha
State President

LETTER FROM FRANK CHIKANE TO P. W. BOTHA

March 18, 1988

Dear Mr. Botha:

I write to you in my capacity as general secretary of the SACC and on behalf of the church leaders of the SACC.

The attack you made on Archbishop Tutu—with regard to the petition presented to you dated the 29th February, the Archbishop's covering letter dated 1st March, and the peaceful march of the church leaders on the 29th February in Cape Town—is of great concern to us.

Archbishop Tutu was one of a large group of church leaders and the clergy who marched. The petition was drawn up and signed by twenty-five church leaders.

We therefore are concerned that you have singled out the Archbishop for your allegations and wish to reiterate that the march of witness and protest and the petition presented to you are actions that were taken by many, and endorsed by an even greater number of church people here and abroad.

The reasons for these actions, both of which were peaceful, were to witness and protest.

a) The actions were meant to *witness* to the vast majority of the people in this country, who are in our parishes, that we the church leaders cannot accept the ungodly acts of oppression of this government.

Thus, a public act, in the form of a march, was a public witness to our constituency. Talks behind closed doors with government leaders have not achieved anything. Church leaders have often come away humiliated and the people they represent are not able to witness these discussions.

The lack of success of such meetings has led many church leaders to believe that such attempts at change are hopeless, especially where those in power are determined at all costs to maintain white domination and apartheid.

b) The *protest* was aimed at the government in a nonviolent, peaceful manner. Our protest was against the *evils* of *apartheid* which we observe and experience in South Africa as part of the "evil in the world." Thus we proclaim to our people, in the context of a day to day oppression and dehumanisation of apartheid, now intensified through the effective bannings of organisations and individuals, that "victory against evil in this world is guaranteed by our Lord."

We are bound to proclaim the gospel in the context of our experience of injustice and oppression in South Africa under the apartheid government. I would like to let you know that the majority of members of our churches have never experienced oppression and brutal suppression of their political expression by Marxists, the ANC, or the SACP, *but* under your government. We stand and will always be against totalitarianism of any kind, irrespective of who is involved and whatever ideological position they hold.

You asked Archbishop Tutu whether his view of evil includes "the struggle on behalf of Christianity, the Christian faith, and freedom of faith and worship, against the forces of godlessness and *Marxism*." In our understanding and experience of the struggle for the Christian faith and freedom of faith and worship in this land, we have to struggle against the forces of godlessness and *apartheid,* for it is the apartheid government that interrupts church services and seeks to control funeral services, all of which are part of the duties and life of the church.

You ask in your letter whether it is not true that the Christian church knows no other power than life and faith, and no other message than the true message of Christ. We say our message is exactly that: We proclaim the message of God's love for the oppressed in this land and our message to them is the message of God: "Have nothing to do with the fruitful deeds of darkness but rather expose them. For it is shameful even to mention what the disobedient do in secret. But everything exposed by the light becomes visible, for it is light that makes everything visible" (Eph. 5:11-13).

We understand our activities to be based on the gospel and that our mandate is from God. Our prophetic mission is God's mission, i.e. to preach the good news of freedom to the poor and oppressed.

It was this tradition which the prophets of Israel took up when they protested against the abuse of power by the kings. Jesus also identifies himself with the poor and the downtrodden.

We feel that this unprecedented attack on the clergy may be paving the way for a state clampdown on the church and its witness to the truth. The church throughout the ages has borne the brunt of such attacks while governments have come and gone.

We therefore pledge ourselves to the gospel of Christ against the forces of evil of this country and we commit ourselves to working for the ushering in of a new order of peace and justice for all; we make that pledge and commitment irrespective of the consequences. To quote the church leaders' statement: "If the state wants to act against the church of God in this country for proclaiming the gospel, then so be it."

Yours sincerely,

Frank Chikane
General Secretary
South African Council of Churches

LETTER FROM P. W. BOTHA TO FRANK CHIKANE

Tuynhuys
Cape Town

March 25, 1988

PERSONAL

The General Secretary
South African Council of Churches
PO Box 4921
Johannesburg
2000

Dear Rev. Chikane:

I hereby acknowledge receipt of your letter of 18 March 1988, which I read with a certain measure of alarm and concern.

I am surprised at your reaction concerning my letter to Archbishop Tutu, which was a reply to the petition as well as to a letter he sent to me when he forwarded the petition to me. In your letter you referred to an attack I was supposed to have made "on Archbishop Tutu, with regard to the petition, the Archbishop's covering letter, and the march of the church leaders," while you also asserted that I "singled out the Archbishop."

I have seldom seen such a flagrant misrepresentation of a situation, and I seriously question your motives in this regard.

Firstly, the only reason why I wrote to Archbishop Tutu was because he wrote to me, because he was asked to do so by those who marched with him. It is as simple as that. I trust that your replying on his behalf does not signify a motion of no confidence in the Archbishop's handling of the matter, but I did note the fact that the SACC apparently no longer believes that the Archbishop can act and speak on its behalf.

Secondly, I did not single out the Archbishop by receiving him in Tuynhuys—I handed the letter to him at a meeting which took place at *his specific request*. He asked for the meeting!

Thirdly, if you read my letter properly, you will also find that I did not single out the Archbishop in that either. On the contrary, I specifically addressed "you and the *others* who were with you on that day"; "*those* who support this petition"; "*those* who *co-signed* the petition"; "*your* individual capac*ities* as mem*bers*." Your allegation is therefore devoid of all truth.

In view of this, and of the general drift of your letter, I wish to address you frankly.

I grew up in an environment where the Lord was served, where the love of God, His Church, and His Word was transferred to me, and which I cherish in my heart to this very day. That is why I strive to conduct my personal life, and my service as State President, according to the principles of the Christian faith.

This government has, in the light of the message of the Bible, gone out of its way to serve the people of this country, to broaden democracy, to remove hurtful and discriminatory legislation and social practices, and to provide for the needs of all on a scale that is found nowhere else on this continent.

The quality of life in South Africa compares favourably with the best in Africa. How do you explain the fact that hundreds of thousands of citizens from neighboring countries flee across our borders to seek food, work, health services, and safety in our country which you so miserably misrepresent?

I have gone out of my way to invite leaders of black communities, and also religious leaders, to co-operate with me in pursuing a just, peaceful, and prosperous future for all in South Africa and our region. Many of them already do so.

It is therefore disturbing that you and others, who claim to represent the Church of Christ and the Word of God, act in the irresponsible way that you do.

You do not hesitate to spread malicious untruths about South Africa here and abroad. You should be fully aware of the numerous misleading statements concerning local support for sanctions and for the ANC, alleged atrocities by the security forces, the treatment of youths, and the fabrication of false testimony for especially the overseas media.

You love and praise the ANC/SACP with its Marxist and atheistic ideology, land mines, bombs, and necklaces perpetrating the most horrendous atrocities imaginable; and you embrace and participate in their call for violence, hatred, sanctions, insurrection and revolution.

In this regard you may recall Archbishop Tutu's statement during a lecture in St. Paul's Cathedral in 1984 when he said: "If the Russians were to come to South Africa today, then most blacks who reject communism as atheistic and materialistic would welcome them as saviours."

You may also recall the Archbishop saying that the aims of the SACC and the ANC are similar; and added in Atlanta, Georgia, in January 1986, that: "We hope one day to hear the leaders of the Western world say we sided with the ANC which sought to change an unjust system peacefully; and were sent into the arms of the struggle because the West abandoned us."

The SACC, in its support of the Kairos Document, apparently regards communism as a myth, and in its acceptance of the Harare Declaration and the Lusaka Statement, expressed support for sanctions, disinvestment, and boycotts against South Africa, and support for the Marxist terrorist movements.

It is alarming that God, and the Church of God which I also love and serve, can be abused and insulted in this manner; that individual members of the clergy who claim to be messengers of God, are in reality messengers of enmity and hatred while parading in the cloth, and hiding behind the structures of the Church; instead of pursuing reformation, they are engaged in the deformation of religion, through the proclamation of false so-called "liberation theology."

At the same time responsible church leaders who proclaim the true Gospel of Christ, lament the fact that they are at times intimidated into a conspiracy of silence by those who have chosen the radical path.

The SACC claims to represent the Christians of South Africa. Yet you are aware that only about 1 percent of your income derives from this country—not even enough to pay your own salary and expenses, while all your activities are financed from abroad. Christians of South Africa are therefore justified to ask: just who do you really represent? I trust that you will admit that there are millions of Christians organized in a multitude of denominations in South Africa who are not members of the SACC, and who reject the road on which the SACC has embarked.

I have noted a frenzy of rumour and expectation regarding possible action by the Government against certain members of the clergy. I see no reason for this, unless they take part in subversive and revolutionary activities. But judging on this reaction in certain circles, it does seem as if some people want it to happen, or have reason to believe that it should happen.

I request you urgently not to abuse the freedom of religion and worship, and the goodwill of the people and the Government of South Africa for the pursuance of secular and revolutionary objectives. In the name of God and in the spirit of true Christianity I call upon you to be messengers of the true Christian religion, and not of Marxism and atheism.

Religious freedom is the cornerstone of proper human rights. It is a well known fact that South Africa is a country which cherishes and safeguards freedom of religion. Even in the armed forces more that one hundred different denominations are actively engaged in the preaching of the Gospel.

In this regard it is ironic that you yourself challenged churches in South Africa to provide ministry to the terrorist movements, while at the same time withdrawing chaplains from the SADF [South African Defence Force]!

I am amazed that you as theologian can compare me and the Government with immoral and godless people referred to in Ephesians 5:11-13, while ignoring Ephesians 4:31: "Let all bitterness, and wrath, and anger, and clamour, and evil speaking be put away from you with all malice"; and also Ephesians 5:9: "For the fruit of the Spirit is in all goodness and righteousness and truth."

In this spirit I call upon the co-operation of all churches and church leaders towards creating peace and goodwill among the peoples of our land, for the benefit of the Church of Christ.

In conclusion I want to put a question to the SACC. We are both confessing that we are followers of Christ in spite of all our human weaknesses. Christ, as far as we know, openly took part in the spreading of the Gospel during the last three years of his life on earth. Can you quote one single instance from the Word of God in which it appears that Christ advocated violence against the State; or led a demonstration against the State; or broke a law of the State?

Yours sincerely,

P. W. Botha
State President

LETTER FROM DESMOND TUTU TO P. W. BOTHA

April 8, 1988

Dear Mr. State President:

Thank you for your letter dated 16 March 1988. I must confess I am surprised that a letter marked "Personal" should have been distributed to Members of Parliament and to the media without the concurrence of its recipient. I thought that there were conventions governing such things.

Since you are a fair-minded person, I am sure you will ensure that my reply will receive the same publicity accorded your letter to me. Certainly I am sure you will ask SABC-TV to give it equally prominent coverage.

Recently you and I had an interview which I had requested for the sole purpose of appealing to you to exercise your prerogative to commute the death sentence of the so-called "Sharpeville Six" and which you then used as an occasion for haranguing me about the Church leaders and our petition. I am distressed that during that interview you appeared to sit loosely to facts.

You had already been reported in an interview with the *Washington Times* as alleging that our petition was drawn up after the march. I tried to correct this erroneous view. But you then proceeded to accuse me of having preached under a flag depicting the hammer and sickle. I denied this accusation. You did not withdraw your extraordinary accusations, but claimed that you had photographs to prove your charge. I challenged you to produce this photographic evidence which I knew was non-existent because I have never been so photographed as you had alleged. I refer to this matter because of the questions in your letter about atheistic Marxism.

I want to state quite categorically that I stand by all that I have done and said in the past concerning the application of the Gospel of Jesus Christ to the situation of injustice and oppression and exploitation which are of the very essence of apartheid, a policy which your government has carried out with ruthless efficiency. My position in this matter is not one of which I am ashamed or for which I would ever want to apologise. I know that I stand in the mainline Christian tradition. I want you to know that I have never listened to Radio Freedom nor do I have the opportunity to read *Sechaba*. My theological position derives from the Bible and from the teaching of the Church. The Bible and the Church predate Marxism and the ANC by several centuries.

May I give you a few illustrations? The Bible teaches that what invests each person with infinite value is not this or that arbitrarily chosen biological attribute, but the fact that each person is created in the image of God (Gen. 1:26). Apartheid, the policy of your government, claims that what makes a person qualify for privilege and political power is that biological irrelevance, the colour of a person's skin and his or her ethnic antecedents. Apartheid says those are what make a person matter. That is clearly at variance with the teaching of the Bible and the teaching of our Lord and Saviour Jesus Christ. Hence the Church's criticism that your apartheid policies are not only unjust and oppressive. They are positively unbiblical, un-Christian, immoral, and evil.

Apartheid says that ultimately people are intended for separation. You have carried out policies enshrined in the Population Registration Act and the Group Areas Act; you have carried out policies of segregated education and health, etc. The Bible teaches quite unequivocally that people are created for fellowship, for togetherness, not for alienation, apartness, enmity, and division (Gen. 2:18; Gen. 11:1-9; 1 Cor. 12:12-13; Rom. 12:3-51; Gal. 3:28; Acts 17:26).

The experience of the United States and the findings of its highest court were that it is in fact impossible to carry out a policy of "separate but equal." The policies of apartheid do not even pretend to seek to embody "separate but equal." Quite unabashedly they are intended to embody "separate and unequal." Just note the grossly unfair distribution of land between black and white or the unequal government expenditure on black and white education. I could multiply the examples.

Apartheid, the policy of your government, is thus shown yet again to be unbiblical, un-Christian, immoral, and evil in its very nature.

I could show that apartheid teaches the fundamental irreconcilability of people because they belong to different races. This is at variance with the central teaching of the Christian faith about the reconciling work of our Lord and Saviour Jesus Christ. "God was in Christ reconciling the world to Himself" declares St. Paul (2 Cor. 5:9), summing up teaching contained in other parts of the New Testament (John 12:32; Eph. 1:10; Eph. 2:14; etc). I could show that in dealing with some human beings as if they were less than created in the image of God and by inflicting untold and unnecessary suffering on them, as through your vicious policies of forced population removals, you have contravened basic ethical tenets. I could provide further evidence that your apartheid policies are unbiblical, un-Christian, immoral, and evil. It is for these and other reasons that our church and other churches have declared apartheid a heresy. I am quite ready to debate this issue with a theologian from your church whom you might care to nominate.

I have not deviated from the teaching of our church on this matter at any point. I enclose copies of the statements issued by my fellow bishops and others showing that they believe I stand in the teaching and tradition of our church. I want to submit respectfully that it is more likely that they would be better judges of the orthodoxy of my position than the State President and his advisors, theological and otherwise.

What we are doing is no innovation when we bring the Word of God as we understand it to bear on the situation in which we are involved. The prophets of old when they declared "Thus saith the Lord . . ." to the rulers and the powerful of their day were our forerunners. They spoke about the need for religion to show its authenticity by how it affected the everyday life of the people and especially by how the rich, the powerful, the privileged, and the rulers dealt with the less privileged, the poor, the hungry, the oppressed, the widow, the orphan, and the alien.

Isaiah said God rejected all religious observances however punctilious and elaborate. He urged worshipers to "Put away the evil of your deeds, away out of my sight. Cease to do evil and learn to do right, pursue justice and champion the oppressed; give the orphan his rights, plead the widow's cause" (Isa. 1:16-17). Elsewhere he claimed that God was not pleased with their religious fasts.

God declared through the prophet, "Is not this what I require of you as a fast: to loose the fetters of injustice, to untie the knots of the yoke, to snap every yoke and set free those who have been crushed? Is it not sharing your food with the hungry, taking the homeless poor into your house, clothing the naked when you meet them and never evading a duty to your kinsfolk?" (Isa. 58:6-7).

Elijah confronted the king about his injustice to Naboth, a nonentity as far as the king was concerned but a person who was championed by God (1 Kings 21); Nathan was not afraid to convict David of his sinfulness (2 Sam. 12). This kind of involvement of religion with politics and the habit of religious leaders to speak into the socio-political and economic situation can be attested to as standard practice in the Bible, which provided our mandate and paradigm.

Our marching orders come from Christ Himself and not from any human being. Our mandate is provided by the Bible and the teaching of the Church, not by any political group or ideology, Marxist or otherwise.

Our Lord Himself, in His first sermon as recorded by St. Luke (Luke 4:16–21), adopted as a description of His programme that which was outlined by Isaiah: "The spirit of the Lord God is upon me because the Lord has anointed me; he has sent me to bring good news to the humble, to bind up the broken-hearted, to proclaim liberty to captives and release to those in prison; to proclaim a year of the Lord's favour and a day of the vengeance of our God" (Isa. 61:1-2). Our Lord stood in the prophetic tradition when He taught what criteria would be used to judge the nations—it would not be through observance of narrowly defined religious duties but by whether they had fed the hungry, clothed the naked, visited the sick and imprisoned, etc. (Matt. 25:31-46).

It is impossible to love God whom one has not seen if one hates the brother whom one has seen, testifies another part of the New Testament (1 John 4:20-21).

The followers of Jesus are constrained by the imperatives of His Gospel to be concerned for those He has called the least of His brethren. The NGK [Dutch Reformed Mission Church] recognised this when it was in the forefront of the struggle for justice for the poor whites as evidenced by the words of Dr. C. D. Brink in a paper delivered at the Volkskongres in 1947: "The aim of the church is to bring about social justice. Justice must be done to the poor and the oppressed, and if the present system does not serve this purpose, the public conscience must be roused to demand another. If the church does not exert itself for justice in society, and together with the help she can offer also be prepared to serve as champion for the cause of the poor, others will do it. The poor have their right today: I do not ask for your charity, but I ask to be given an opportunity to live a life of human dignity."

We are law-abiding. Good laws make human society possible. When laws are unjust then Christian tradition teaches that they do not oblige obedience. Our Lord broke not just human law but what was considered more serious, He broke God's law in order to meet human need—as when He broke the law of the Sabbath observance (John 5:8-14). He paid due regard to the secular ruler in the person of Pontius Pilate but subsequently engaged in a defiance of that secular authority when He refused to answer his questions (Mark 15:3-5).

It is a hallowed tradition of direct nonviolent action such as we engaged in when we tried to process to Parliament. We were mindful too of what the apostles said to the Jewish Sanhedrin, that obedience to God takes precedence of obedience to human beings (Acts 4:19; 5:29).

We accept wholeheartedly St. Paul's teaching in Romans 13—that we should submit ourselves to earthly rulers. Their authority however is not absolute. They themselves also stand under God's judgment as His servants. They are meant to instill fear only in those who do wrong, holding no terror for those who do right (Rom. 13:3-4). The ruler is God's servant to do the subjects good (Rom. 13:4). The ruler rules for the benefit of the ruled. That comes not out of our political manifesto but from the Holy Scriptures. The corollary is that you must not submit yourself to a ruler who subverts your good. That is why we admire those who oppose unjust regimes, e.g. totalitarian communist governments. The Bible teaches that governments can become beasts in the symbolic language of the book of Revelation (Rev. 13). Not too many governments nor their apologists who use Romans 13 with glee are quite so enthusiastic about its full implications nor of Revelation 13.

I am sure you could not have been serious when you quoted a passage allegedly from Radio Freedom in which you underline certain words, such as *church, liberation struggle, justice,* and then went on to suggest that because our petition uses similar words there must be a sinister connection between us and the ANC. If a communist were to say, "Water makes you wet," would you say, "No, water does not make you wet," for fear that people would accuse you of being a communist? I would have thought our discussion was at a slightly higher level.

I told you in my interview that I support the ANC in its objectives to establish a nonracial, democratic South Africa; but I do not support its methods. That is a statement I have made in the Supreme Court in Pretoria and on other occasions. My views have never been clandestine. You appointed the Eloff Commission to investigate the SACC when I was still its General Secretary. Your Security Police investigated my personal life and looked into my bank accounts and tried to discredit me in their evidence before the Commission. They were unable to find anything of which to accuse me. Not even Craig Williamson could produce evidence that I held different views to those I had expressed in public. You know I went to Lusaka twice last year. I tried to persuade the ANC to suspend the armed struggle; that is a matter of public record.

I am committed to work for a nonracial, just, and democratic South Africa. I reject atheistic Marxism as I reject apartheid, which I find equally abhorrent and evil. Transfer of power to the people of South Africa means exactly that. The latest apartheid Constitution cannot by any stretch of imagination be described as democratic when it excludes 73 percent of the people of South Africa from any meaningful participation in the political decision making process. I long for and have dedicated myself to work for a South Africa where all South Africans are South Africans, citizens in an undivided South Africa, not one that is balkanised into unviable bantustan homelands. When you are a citizen you share through the exercise of your vote in the political decision making process either directly or through duly elected representatives. Since 1976 I have appealed to the government to heed our cri de coeur. I have said nobody in their right senses expected these real changes to happen overnight. You yourself can bear me out that when an SACC leaders' delegation met you and your Cabinet colleagues in 1980, I again said that if you did something dramatic then I would be among the first to say to our people, "Hold it. Give them a chance, now they are talking real change." Then I said, "Declare your commitment to a common citizenship for all South Africans in an undivided South Africa; abolish the pass laws; stop immediately all forced population removals and establish a uniform education policy." That was eight years ago. How much time has been wasted and how many lives have been lost trying to beautify apartheid through cosmetic improvements when the pillars of a vicious system still remain firmly in place.

I would say if you were to lift the State of Emergency, unban all our political organisations, release all detainees and political prisoners, and permit exiles to return, and then say you would be ready to sit down with the authentic representatives and leaders of every section of our society to negotiate the dismantling of apartheid and drawing up of a new constitution, I would say to our people, "Please give him a chance. He is talking real change." Your apartheid policies are leading our beautiful land to disaster. We love South Africa passionately. Our black fathers fought against the Nazis for it; many Afrikaners being pro-Nazi at the time refused to support the war effort, and many who wore the uniform of the Union Defence Force used to be turned away from NGK church services.

We long for the day when black and white will live amicably and harmoniously together in the new South Africa.

Kindly confirm whether you include me in the paragraph in your letter to the Reverend Frank Chikane which reads: "You love and praise the ANC/SACP with its Marxist and atheistic ideology, land mines, bombs, and necklaces perpetrating the most horrendous atrocities imaginable; and you embrace and participate in their call for violence, hatred, sanctions, insurrection, and revolution, . . ." because as supporting evidence you then quote what I said in St. Paul's Cathedral, London.

I want to state the obvious—that I am a Christian religious leader; by definition that surely means I reject communism and Marxism as atheistic and materialistic. I try to work for the extension of the Kingdom of God which will ultimately have rulers such as the ones described in Isaiah 11:1-9 and in Psalm 72:1-4 and 12-14:

> O God, endow the king with thy own justice,
> and give thy righteousness to a king's son,
> that he may judge thy people rightly and deal out
> justice to the poor and suffering.
> May the hills and mountains afford the people
> peace and prosperity in righteousness.
> He shall give judgement for the suffering
> and help those of the people that are needy;
> he shall crush the oppressor.

> For he shall rescue the needy from their rich oppressors,
> the distressed who have no protector.
> May he have pity on the needy and the poor,
> deliver the poor from death;
> may he redeem them from oppression and violence
> and may their blood be precious in his eyes.

I work for God's Kingdom. For whose Kingdom do you work with your apartheid policy? I pray for you as I do for your ministerial colleagues, every day by name.

God bless you.

Yours sincerely,

Desmond

Glossary

AFRIKAANS—A dialect of the Dutch language spoken by Afrikaners in South Africa.

AFRIKANERS—White South Africans of Dutch descent who established the apartheid system. Afrikaners make up 60 percent of the white population.

ANC (African National Congress)—South African liberation movement founded in 1912 to struggle for a free and just South Africa. Banned by the government and forced underground in 1961.

APARTHEID—South Africa's system of legalized racism. Apartheid denies all civil and human rights to the black majority, and ensures the supremacy of whites.

BANNING—A form of house arrest by which the government silences its critics. Banned individuals cannot be published or quoted, and their movements are restricted.

BANTU—White South Africa's racist term for black people, the majority of the population.

BANTUSTANS—Name for barren wastelands making up only 13 percent of South Africa's land; the South African government has declared these are the only places where the black majority can live permanently.

BLACK CONSCIOUSNESS MOVEMENT—A movement that stresses pride in African heritage and that insists that blacks must take the initiative in their struggle for freedom. It was banned by the South African government.

BLACK SPOT—Land in rural areas occupied by blacks, sometimes for generations, in "whites only" areas of South Africa. These communities are the first target of forced removals.

BLACK TOWNSHIP—The "blacks only" sections of urban areas of South Africa. Townships are far from jobs, are overcrowded, and have poor housing, little electricity and running water, and no sewage systems.

DIVESTMENT—The withdrawal of funds from corporations and banks which support apartheid by doing business in or with South Africa.

FORCED REMOVALS—The South African police's practice of dragging blacks off their land, often at gunpoint, and then bulldozing communities declared to be in "white" areas. Over 3.5 million blacks have been forcibly removed since 1960.

FRELIMO (Front for the Liberation of Mozambique) — Governing party in Mozambique which freed the nation from Portuguese rule in 1975.

FRONTLINE STATES — Neighboring countries to South Africa that represent a united front against apartheid. These states include: Angola, Botswana, Mozambique, Tanzania, Zambia, and Zimbabwe.

HOMELAND — South African government's term for portions of land designated for blacks; same as bantustan.

LESOTHO — A small country completely surrounded by South Africa.

MIGRANT LABORERS — Those forced to leave their homes and families in rural bantustans to find employment in urban centers of "white" South Africa.

MNR (Mozambique National Resistance) — South Africa-supported terrorist group infamous for murder.

MPLA (Popular Movement for the Liberation of Angola) — The governing party in Angola which freed the nation from Portuguese rule in 1975.

NAMIBIA — The country which South Africa's military has occupied since 1915. In December 1988, a peace treaty was signed that called for the removal of South African troops from this country. Namibia was formerly called South West Africa.

NATIONAL PARTY — The ruling party in South Africa, it is led by the Afrikaners. It came to power in 1948 on a platform of white supremacy and legalized apartheid, and stripped blacks of all rights.

NKOMATI PEACE ACCORD — By supporting the MNR and carrying out sabotage against its neighbors, South Africa has forced Mozambique to sign agreements which forbid it to support the ANC and PAC militarily. South Africa has not carried out its promise to end support for the MNR mercenaries.

PAC (Pan Africanist Congress) — South African liberation movement founded in 1959, based on black nationalism. Banned by the government in 1961.

PASSBOOK — A document all blacks formerly had to carry at all times. Whites were not required to have one. Failure to carry a passbook resulted in arrest and imprisonment for blacks.

PASS LAWS — Laws which control the movement of blacks. These laws forbid blacks to live in "white" areas and help the government control workers.

PRETORIA — The capital city of South Africa; also refers to the South African government.

RACE CLASSIFICATION—Apartheid laws divide South Africans into four racial groups: Africans—people of African descent (72 percent of the population); coloreds—people of mixed race (9 percent of the population); whites—people of European descent (16 percent of the population); and Asians—mostly people of Indian descent (about 3 percent of the population).

SHARPEVILLE MASSACRE—On March 21, 1960, South African police shot and killed sixty-nine blacks who were peacefully demonstrating against pass laws.

SOWETO—A black township of Johannesburg. Over two million blacks live in the impoverished township.

SOWETO UPRISING—On June 16, 1976, South African police gunned down students in Soweto who were peacefully demonstrating against apartheid education. This began a series of protests and clashes with police around the country; one thousand people are estimated to have been killed.

SUBSISTENCE FARMING—Raising only enough food to meet basic needs. Most people who live in bantustans cannot grow enough food to maintain good health.

SWAPO (South West Africa People's Organization)—The liberation movement fighting to free Namibia since 1966.

UNITA (National Union for the Total Independence of Angola)—Pro-Western forces of Angola fighting to overthrow the government of Angola; often supported by the South African military.

The above glossary is an updated version of that by the Washington Office on Africa, 110 Maryland Ave, NE, Washington, DC 20002; (202) 546–7961.

Resources

ORGANIZATIONS

American Committee on Africa, 198 Broadway, Room 402, New York, NY 10038; (212) 962–1210.

The Interfaith Committee on Corporate Responsibility/Corporate Information Center, 475 Riverside Drive, New York, NY 10115.

International Defence and Aid Fund, Box 17, Cambridge, MA 02138.

The National Council of Churches, Africa Office, 475 Riverside Drive, New York, NY 10115; (212) 870–2645.

TransAfrica, 545 8th Street, SE, Washington, DC 20003; (202) 547–2550.

The United Nations Centre against Apartheid, Room 3580, U.N. Plaza, New York, NY 10017; (212) 754–5291.

The Washington Office on Africa, 110 Maryland Avenue, NE, Washington, DC 20002; (202) 546–7961.

PERIODICALS

Africa News, biweekly magazine, published by Africa News Service, Box 3851, Durham, NC 27705.

Focus on Political Repression in Southern Africa, bimonthly journal, published by the International Defence and Aid Fund for Southern Africa, U.S. Committee, Box 17, Cambridge, MA 02138.

BOOKS

On South Africa in General

Biko, Steve. *I Write What I Like.* Ed. Aelred Stubbs. San Francisco: Harper & Row, 1978.

Bernstein, Hilda. *For Their Triumphs and Their Tears: Women in Apartheid South Africa.* Cambridge: International Defence and Aid Fund, 1975.

de Gruchy, John. *The Church Struggle in South Africa.* Grand Rapids: Eerdmans, 1979.

de Gruchy, John, ed. *Cry Justice!* Maryknoll, N.Y.: Orbis Books, 1986. Prayers, meditations, and readings from South Africa.

Friedman, Julian R. *Basic Facts on the Republic of South Africa and the Policy of Apartheid.* New York: U.N. Centre against Apartheid, 1977.

Hope, Anne. *Torch in the Night.* New York and Washington: Friendship Press and The Center of Concern, 1988. Worship resources from South Africa.

Litvak, Lawrence, Robert DeGrasse, and Kathleen McTigue. *South Africa: Foreign Investment and Apartheid.* Washington: Institute for Policy Studies, 1978.

Logan, Willis H., ed. *The Kairos Covenant: Standing with South African Christians.* Oak Park, Ill., and New York: Meyer-Stone Books and Friendship Press, 1988.

Luckhardt, Ken, and Brenda Wall. *Working for Freedom: Black Trade Union Development in South Africa.* Geneva: World Council of Churches, 1981.

Mandela, Nelson. *No Easy Walk to Freedom.* Ed. Heinemann, 1965. Collection of Mandela's speeches, articles, and addresses to the court during his trials in the 1950s and 1960s.

Rogers, Barbara. *Divide and Rule: South Africa's Bantustans.* Cambridge: International Defence and Aid Fund, 1980.

Seidman, Judy. *Facelift Apartheid: South Africa after Soweto.* Cambridge: International Defence and Aid Fund, 1980.

Troup, Freda. *Forbidden Pastures: Education under Apartheid.* Cambridge: International Defence and Aid Fund.

Wilson, Monica, and Leonard Thompson, eds. *The Oxford History of South Africa.* Vols. 1 and 2. New York: Oxford University Press, 1971.

Woods, Donald. *Biko.* New York: Random, 1979.

Woods, Donald, and Mike Bostock. *Apartheid: A Graphic Guide.* New York: Henry Holt and Company, 1988.

Women under Apartheid. Cambridge: International Defence and Aid Fund, 1981.

By Allan Boesak

Black and Reformed. Maryknoll, N.Y.: Orbis Books, 1984.

Comfort and Protest. Philadelphia: Westminster, 1987.

Farewell to Innocence. Maryknoll, N.Y.: Orbis Books, 1977.

The Finger of God. Maryknoll, N.Y.: Orbis Books, 1982.

If This Is Treason, I Am Guilty. Grand Rapids: Eerdmans, 1987.

Walking on Thorns. Grand Rapids: Eerdmans, 1984.
When Prayer Makes News. Philadelphia: Westminster, 1986. Edited with Charles Villa-Vicencio.

By Frank Chikane
No Life of My Own. Maryknoll, N.Y.: Orbis Books, 1989.

By Beyers Naudé
Hope for Faith. Geneva and Grand Rapids: World Council of Churches and Eerdmans, 1986.
Not without Honour. Johannesburg: Ravan Press, 1962.

About Beyers Naudé
Mcleod, Bryan G. *Naudé, Prophet to South Africa.* Atlanta: John Knox, 1978.
Villa-Vicencio, Charles, and John de Gruchy. *Resistance and Hope.* Grand Rapids: Eerdmans, 1985.

By Desmond Tutu
Crying in the Wilderness. Grand Rapids: Eerdmans, 1982.
The Divine Intention. Braamfontein: SACC, 1982.
Hope and Suffering. Grand Rapids: Eerdmans, 1984.
The Words of Desmond Tutu. New York: Newmarket, 1989.

About Desmond Tutu
Bentley, Judith. *Archbishop Tutu.* Milwaukee: G. Stevens, 1988.
De Boulay, Shirley. *Tutu.* Grand Rapids: Eerdmans, 1988.
Green, Carol. *Desmond Tutu, Bishop of Peace.* Chicago: Children Press, 1986.
Tlhagale, Buti, and Itumeleng Mosala. *Hammering Swords into Ploughshares.* Grand Rapids and Trenton: Eerdmans and Africa World Press, 1987.
Wepman, Dennis. *Desmond Tutu.* New York: F. Watts, 1989.

By Charles Villa-Vicencio
Apartheid Is a Heresy. Grand Rapids: Eerdmans, 1983. Edited with John de Gruchy.
Between Christ and Caesar. Grand Rapids: Eerdmans, 1986.
Theology and Violence. Grand Rapids: Eerdmans, 1988.
Trapped in Apartheid. Maryknoll, N.Y.: Orbis Books, 1988.
When Prayer Makes News. Philadelphia: Westminster, 1986. Edited with Allan Boesak.